THE ROAD TO
COMPOSTELA

The Road to Compostela

Rob Neillands

MOORLAND PUBLISHING

British Library Cataloguing in
Publication Data

Neillands, Rob.
  The road to Compostela.
  1. Christian pilgrims and pilgrimages
  — Spain — Santiago de Compostela
  2. France — Description and travel
  3.Spain, Northern — Description and
  travel
  Rn: Robin Hunter Neillands
  I. Title
  914.4   DC29.3

© Rob Neillands 1985
ISBN 0 86190 059 6

Printed in the UK by
Dotesios (Printers) Ltd,
Bradford-on-Avon, Wiltshire.
Published by
Moorland Publishing Co Ltd,
Station Street,
Ashbourne, Derbyshire,
DE6 1DE England.
Tel: (0335) 44486

Contents

This book is dedicated, with great affection, to the Viallard family, Jacques, Isabelle, Marin, Gabriel and Armand, and to Eve Livet, the Lady from Lyon.

'*Le voyage a St Jacques est toujours une aventure*'

'I said to the man who stood at the Gate of the Year, "Give me a light that I might tread safely into the unknown". And he replied, "Go out into the darkness, and put your hand into the Hand of God. That shall be to you brighter than a light, and safer than a known way." '

M. L. Haskins

'The reward of a thing well done is to have done it.'

Emerson

Acknowledgements

A great many people have helped or encouraged the writing of this book, so my thanks to Pat Quaife, Mary Remnant, Peter Johnson and all members of the Confraternity of St James in England; to Pauline Hallam of the French National Tourist Office and Lucinda Bartelot of the Spanish National Tourist Office; Canon Griffiths of St Peter's Church, Marlow-on-Thames; Shona Crawford-Poole, travel editor of *The Times*; Mademoiselle J. Warcollier and her colleagues of Le Société des Amis de St Jacques, Paris; Madame Debril of St Jean Pied de Port; Señor Ballesteros and Señor Suso of Santiago de Compostela; the London Library; and as usual to Estelle Huxley who holds the fort when I am away enjoying myself.

Preface

This is the story of a journey. According to Andrew Boorde, who passed this way in the sixteenth century, the old pilgrim trail that leads across France and Spain to the shrine of St James at Compostela in Galicia is 'the greatest journey that any Englishman mae goe' and having made the trip by bicycle in the hot, dry summer of 1982, I wouldn't disagree with that. The Road to Compostela is also an adventure, but an adventure on a human scale, always exciting, if never exactly easy.

I chose to make this journey down the Road from Le Puy on a bicycle, and it seems wise to point out at the start that I am not a passionate cyclist. Readers expecting a cog and sprocket-crammed narrative are doomed to disappointment. That said, the bicycle is the perfect steed for such a journey and I recommend any reader contemplating this journey to consider making it on a bike. The miles slip past comfortably at an average of forty or fifty a day, and there is plenty of time to see the sights. After all, those who go by cycle or on foot are 'true pilgrims'; they experience the heat, the dust, even the danger of the pilgrimage, they share the full experience and enjoy the fellowship of other pilgrims on the Road.

When it came to writing this book, I had a problem. It is hard to prevent any travel book leading the reader in and out of church doors, especially in a book concerned with a pilgrimage, but over a month this can be tedious. The story of the Road to Compostela is fascinating but complex and, anyway, my object is not so much to retell an old tale but to encourage my readers to make the journey for themselves. In the end I decided to avoid excessive detail, touch lightly on those matters requiring complicated explanations, and refer those in search of further enlightenment to the bibliography.

This then is the simple story of how one Englishman went down the Road to Compostela, a trail pioneered by the Bishop of Le Puy in the year 950, and followed by millions of pilgrims from all over Europe in the thousand years since. Anyone who 'takes the cockle' and sets out for Compostela, therefore becomes, whether they know it or not, a part of history, for very little has changed along the Road; the sun beats down as fiercely, the hills are just as high, the *meseta* of Castile as dusty and waterless as it ever was. Every step along the Road becomes a step back into the past.

My most enduring memories, though, are not of the heat or the hills. I mostly remember what my fellow pilgrim, Jacques Viallard, called the fellowship of the Road, without which this journey would either never have been completed or been much less fun.

So, pilgrim, go forth; take the cockle and so set out for Compostela. The journey may surprise you, and you, yourself.

Ultreja e sus eja
Deus adjava nos

Mallorca 1985

Introduction

The Road to Compostela is not like other roads. It comes out of the past, a pilgrim route through the countries of Western Christendom, and any traveller setting out across Europe for the Shrine of St James in Galicia is travelling in two dimensions, forward through space and backward through time.

Pilgrims have been travelling to Compostela for a thousand years and more, but it seems necessary to begin this account of my own travels by stating that I am not an especially religious person. On my return from Compostela I quickly discovered that when you tell people that you have just ridden your bike for a thousand miles across France and Spain to the Shrine of the Apostle, their reaction is immediate and obvious. A look of discomfort clouds the face, a feeling of unease colours the conversation, and the atmosphere becomes a little strained.

If an explanation is needed, the simplest one is that I am a lover of travel and history, particularly medieval history. No one can be very interested in that period without becoming concerned with the affairs of the Church which, during the Middle Ages, was greatly preoccupied with the organisation of Crusades and pilgrimages.

That apart, I earn my living as a travel writer and since the Road to Compostela is one of the oldest and most interesting journeys in Europe, and the subject of one of the world's first guidebooks, written as long ago as 1149, the idea of a journey down the Road excited my professional, as well as my private interest. I also thought it might be fun.

Mankind has always been concerned with pilgrimages, with the need to go on a journey. The pilgrimage is not even a specifically Christian phenomenon; Muslims go to Mecca, Hindus to the Ganges, and Jews will tell each other by way of a promise, 'Next year in Jerusalem'. The idea of the pilgrimage, of a voyage to a place connected with the spirit, seems to touch a chord in human nature, while the pilgrimage itself often serves as an allegory, as an example of Man's journey through this life towards . . . what? That depends, it would seem, on the journey, but John Bunyan and Geoffrey Chaucer, to name but two, have found a source of inspiration in the pilgrimage.

As far as Christians are concerned, pilgrimages have a long and enduring history. Pilgrims were arriving in Jerusalem by the third century AD, inspired by the work of St Helena, one of the earliest and most successful archaeologists who discovered the relics of the Crucifixion. These early pilgrimages were encouraged by St Jerome, who lived in Bethlehem; '. . . not for themselves but for the honour of those whose faith they witness', although St Jerome soon had second thoughts. 'It is not locality but character that avails' he said later. 'The gates of Heaven are as open in Britain as in Jerusalem.' The Seventh Council of the Church, which met at Nicaea in 787, insisted that every new church should be endowed with a holy relic, and such relics soon provided the focal point for many pilgrimages. It has been said, with some accuracy, that the true religion of the Middle Ages was founded on the cult of relics.

By the year 1000 the Christian world had established three main pilgrimages, to Jerusalem, to Rome, and to the shrine of St James at Santiago de Compostela in north-west Spain. Later on there were to be others, to Canterbury and Walsingham, then to Fatima and Lourdes, but the original three have endured to the present day, and none has retained so much of the original spirit as the one to Compostela, not least because while other pilgrimages were entirely concerned with the shrine, the pilgrims to Compostela were almost equally concerned with the journey, with the Road itself.

The year of the first millenium is a good point to start this story, for it was widely believed at the time that the world would end in the thousandth year after Christ. This calamity was foretold in the *Book of Revelation:*

An angel came down from Heaven and laid hold on the dragon which is the Devil and Satan and bound him a thousand years.

And cast him into a bottomless pit that he should deceive the nations no more till the thousand years should be fulfilled: and after that he must be loosed a little season.

Rev 20:1-3

Such events as the coming of the Northmen were cited as evidence of approaching doom, but when the year 1000 passed and nothing happened, a new spirit arose, a sudden blossoming of hope, not unlike that of the Renaissance and, to quote a Cluniac monk, Randolf Glaben, 'The world threw off the old rags and put on the shining white garments of churches'.

The great days of the pilgrimage were between 1000 and 1500, when many difficulties faced the pilgrims, wherever the chosen destination. Pilgrims to Jerusalem faced the corsair-infested seas, and after the brief success of the First Crusade in 1099, the Holy City fell again to the Saracens in 1187. For much of this time Rome was in ruins, the Church was riven by schism and for a long period the Pope himself resided at Avignon. There remained the Road to Compostela. Compostela attracted the Christian pilgrim for several reasons. It was far enough away, and difficult enough to reach to provide those necessary elements of endurance and adventure that all true pilgrimages must entail. It lay in the land of Spain, a mysterious country then locked in struggle with the Moor.

Finally, the Road to St James was, and is, well supplied with other sights and shrines, each well worth a visit, each luring the pilgrim on a little further, so that whatever the difficulties, a little faith would take him on to the next shrine, or 'place of obligation', gaining a place in Heaven even if he died on the Way. Medieval man saw nothing odd in this. His world was simpler and no more terrible than our own, and at least he had his faith to keep him going:

These all died in faith, not having received the promises, but having perceived them far off, and were persuaded of them and embraced them and confessed that they were strangers and pilgrims of the earth.

Hebrews 13

St James as a pilgrim

St James, or Santiago, or St Jacques, or St Yakob, the patron
of Spain, the first apostle to be martyred, was an active saint,
appearing frequently to encourage or admonish his early
followers, and his cult was, and remains, widespread. James
the Greater, son of Zebedee, brother of John, called
Bonarges, the 'Son of Thunder' because of his loud voice, is
credited with carrying the gospel into Spain. Spain, or

Hispania, was one of the great provinces of the Roman Empire, so that much is quite possible. The legend of St James has it that after evangelising the peninsula, he returned home to Judaea in AD44, and was executed by Herod. 'The king stretched forth his hand to vex the church and killed James, the brother of John, with the sword.'

Then, according to one account, his followers, 'accompanied by an angel of the Lord, took the body to Jaffa, where they found ready a miraculous ship, which bore them to the harbour of Iria Flavia on the coast of Galicia in Spain.' As this ship approached the shore, those on board saw a man riding a horse along the beach, which took fright at the cortège and plunged into the sea to reappear with horse and rider covered in white scallop-shells, which then became the emblem of St James. Galicia was ruled at the time by a pagan queen, Queen Lupa, so James's followers concealed the body somewhere close to the coast, and there the apostle rested for over eight hundred years.

Now, what can one say about all this? In matters of faith, it is not so much the truth that matters, but what is believed, and these tales form part of the story of Santiago and provide the start of the legend. This picks up the story again during a time of trial. During those eight hundred years while the saint slept, the Roman Empire rose and fell. The Visigoths arrived in the Iberian peninsula, to take over the Imperial possessions, only to fall in their turn before a more enduring conqueror, Islam. The Moors crossed the straits by Gibraltar in 711. By 730 they had overrun the peninsula, and crossed the Pyrenees, and would probably have conquered all of Western Europe but for their defeat by Charles Martel outside Poitiers in 732. They then returned south of the Pyrenees, established the Caliphate of Spain , or *Al-Andaluz,* in 756, and settled down to enjoying their conquest. This conquest, however, was not quite complete.

There remained a small pocket of Christian resistance in the mountains of Cantabrica and Asturias, a small Christian outpost under the leadership of a great patriot, Pelayo. In 718 he had inflicted a small but significant defeat on the Moors, at the battle of Covadongo, and his grandson, Alphonso II, still ruled precariously in the Asturias from 791 until 842. In the year 813, St James rose again, and came to his assistance.

The discovery of the apostle's tomb is credited to a hermit, Pelagro, who was drawn towards the site of the saint's grave by a great star in the sky, one surrounded by many little stars, a veritable 'field of stars', which hovered over a particular spot. On Sunday 25 July, the feast of St James the Apostle, they discovered a sarcophagus, covered by a stone slab, in which lay the severed head and body of St James.

King Alphonso rushed to the site, at what became known as *Campus Stellae,* the 'Field of Stars', and built the first church over the spot; even while this was being built, the good news of the saint's re-emergence was spreading across Christendom. Charlemagne and his paladins were among the first pilgrims, the knights and pilgrims who followed brought arms and assistance to the hard-pressed Christian kingdoms, and the Moors were discomfited. In 846 the saint appeared at the battle of Clavijo in his new role of Matamoros, the Moor-slayer, leading the heavenly host to help the armies of Spain. A tax to support the shrine at Compostela was levied throughout the land and not actually abolished until 1835. St James continued to inspire the Spanish armies throughout the *Reconquista* and cities dedicated to St James dot the old Spanish Empire, from Chile to Cuba, but whatever the long term outcome, we can leave the story there for a while. St James had reappeared at a crucial moment, a fortuitious occurrence no doubt, but in the nick of time to save the fortunes of Christian Spain. In the next two hundred years, his shrine had its ups and downs. The Northmen sacked Compostela in 968, and the Caliph Almanzor descended on the town in 997, but though he razed the buildings to the ground and carried the bells of the church back to Cordoba where, once inverted, they served as lamps in the Great Mosque, even he spared the shrine of the Apostle. From the moment of discovery in 813, the pilgrimage to Santiago began, and has not ceased to this very day.

As to why this pilgrimage lives when so many have faded, the question is answered by the words of the historian Geoffrey Bibby: 'In his heart, every archaeologist knows why he digs; that what is past may not be lost for ever; that something may be salvaged from the wreck of ages'; and so it is still, for even amateur historians. The Road to Compostela lives because it has maintained a continuum from the Dark Ages, through the *Reconquista,* that long struggle of Christian versus Moor, through the Reformation that stamped out much of the pilgrim traffic, through wars and floods and famine. The flow to Compostela has faltered, dried almost to a trickle, but never completely stopped. The Road to Compostela appeals because it is a piece of living history, as valid today as it ever was. It was built on legend, even superstition, but the pilgrimage to St James was necessary for the survival of Spain. Finally, right from the earliest days the pilgrimage to Compostela was organised.

It is important to discard many romantic notions of the period and realise that to the medieval man and woman, a pilgrimage could be, and usually was, much more than an expression of faith. It could be many things, a penance, a plea for assistance, an act of thanksgiving, a punishment or, more often than not, simply a holiday. If Chaucer's Wife of Bath were alive today, she would closely resemble one of those blue-rinsed American ladies who tour the world with tartan luggage, remarking that 'If this is Windsor it must be Tuesday'. She had been, she claims, 'Thrice to Jerusalem, at Rome, at Boloyne, and in Galice at Seynt Jame', a veritable tourist. The point, then and now, is that the pilgrimage need not be serious, or approached with awe. The Road to Compostela has its own dynamic and survives because of it into an increasingly secular age.

The organisation of the pilgrimage to Compostela owes its success to various people, but most notably to Archbishop Gelmirez, who ruled in Compostela around 1100, and to the monks of Cluny. Gelmirez used the pilgrimage to promote the interests of his bishopric, and attract arms and money into Spain. The Cluniacs saw the pilgrimage to Santiago as a means of furthering men to assist the Spanish Church in the long struggle of the *Reconquista.* They built hospices along the way to shelter the pilgrims, they encouraged the building of roads and bridges, they founded pilgrimage churches and endowed them with powerful relics, as focal points of interest to encourage pilgrims along the way. To strike a modern parallel, the Cluniacs served the pilgrim rather as Holiday Inns or Trust House Forte serve the traveller today.

The parallels do not stop here. One of the world's first guide books is about the pilgrimage to Compostela, written, or at least edited, by Ameri Picaud, a monk from Parthenay-le-Vieux in Poitou in 1140. His book, the *Liber Sancti Jacobi,* forms one of a five-volume work known collectively as the *Codex Calixtinus,* which recounts the life and legends of St James, and gives a detailed and still quite useful guide to the Road to Compostela. I followed Picaud's guide across Spain from the Pyrénées to Compostela, and remarked almost daily how little had changed.

The background to this journey, and the legends which surround it, are so many and complex that I will leave the story there for a while and pick up one of the enduring factors, the Road itself. There were, and still are, four roads across France which lead to Compostela, coming from Paris, Vézelay, Le Puy and St Giles. To these, English pilgrims could add the road from Southampton or Bristol to Soulac on the Gironde, and begin their journey by travelling south to the Pyrénées across the Duchy of Aquitaine which, until 1453, was a possession of the English crown. The Pyrénées could be crossed into Spain by two passes, through Roncesvalles or the Somport, and all the roads finally come to together at Puente la Reina in Navarre. From here all the pilgrims travelled together across the country of Castile to Lèon, into Galicia, and on to the good city of the Apostle, an activity which soon attracted the curiosity of the Moors.

Abu Edhari, a Moorish writer, drew up a report on the Santiago pilgrimage for his master Almanzor in 996. He described Compostela as 'San Yakob . . . the great and holy city of the Christians. They come to it as pilgrims in great numbers, and from the most distant parts.'

They still do. Every summer, as the green leaf turns and the heat starts to shimmer across the vineyards of France or the grainfields of Navarre, the Road to Compostela comes alive again. Slowly, a trickle at first, but never a flood, the pilgrims begin to move along the Road, all aiming to arrive in Compostela for the Feast of St James, 25 July. A host of people, young and old, devout and disinterested, Christian or pagan, good and bad, sweep west along this great road which pilgrims have travelled for a thousand years, and in doing so they become, whether they know it or not, a part of history.

This is part of the fascination of the Road for lovers of history. It gives a sense of continuity, of carrying something forward from the past. The pilgrims maintain a tradition, simply by going on a journey through a landscape planted with historic places and peopled by historic figures. Travel the Road to Compostela and you may see, or suffer on, the vasts of the Aubrac; or in crossing the high hills to the shrine of Ste Foy at Conques; on then, to see the red city of Toulouse, and pass through the fortress cities of Aquitaine; then cross the wild Pyrénées to Pamplona in the dancing country of the Basques in time to run with the bulls during the San Firman festival; then turn west to Castile and Léon, forcing a passage across the burning plains to the green and misty mountains of Galicia. A traveller would have to be very short on soul indeed not to find the Road to Compostela entrancing.

Then there are the people; pass through Roncesvalles where Roland fell. Here at Viana lies the neglected dust of Cesare Borgia. On to Burgos where lies Rodrigo Diez de Vivar, better known to history as El Cid. All about you flows the present pilgrim stream, chattering or laughing, dour and determined, pushing on steadily down this Road that quickly comes to form a major part of their lives. This Road to Compostela, as I have said, is not like other roads. It flows out of the past certainly, covering time as well as distance, but the Road itself remains the constant link. For other pilgrims or pilgrimages, the shrine at the end is the objective, but the attraction of the Road to Santiago was and remains, the Road itself.

*　　*　　*

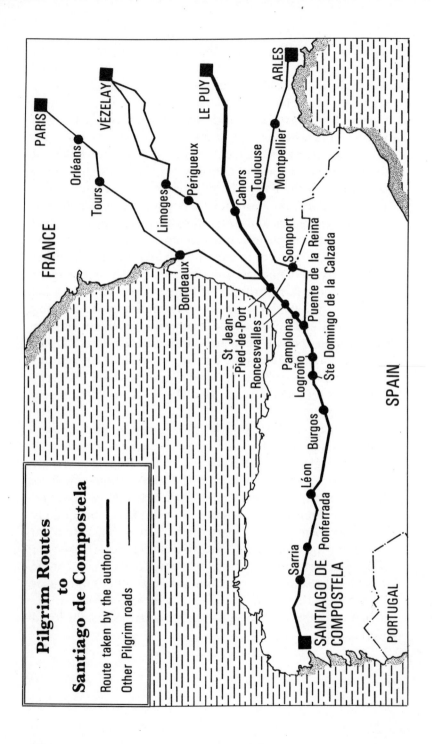

Pilgrim Routes
to
Santiago de Compostela

Route taken by the author
Other Pilgrim roads

FRANCE

PARIS
Orléans
Tours
VÉZELAY
Limoges
Périgueux
LE PUY
Cahors
Toulouse
ARLES
Montpellier
Bordeaux
Somport
Puente de la Reina
St Jean-Pied-de-Port
Roncesvalles
Pamplona
Logroño
Ste Domingo de la Calzada
Burgos
Léon
Ponferrada
Sarria
SANTIAGO DE COMPOSTELA
SPAIN
PORTUGAL

There are four roads to Compostela. I chose to ride the one from Le Puy in the Auvergne, partly because many of the more interesting places lay on that route, mainly because it is the most difficult, and a little difficulty seemed essential, for to be a 'true pilgrim' you have to sweat and this brings me to the bike. A bicycle, a 'push-bike', is as close as I could get to the horse, and it provided me with plenty of that essential pilgrim essence, good honest sweat, but having disposed of the religious mania canard, we had better dispose here of the word 'pilgrim'. To the unreconstructed, the word conjures up a picture of someone sincere in sandals. I use it here to describe someone who, as is proper, makes a journey to Compostela at the expense of some little effort, by foot, on horseback or, as in my case, on a bicycle. Traditionally, the 'true pilgrims' travelled on foot, and this way was considered meritorious, at least by the rich, who regarded it as an act of humility just to get off their horses. The poor, who had no choice and were humble anyway, had to do without this extra act of virtue, and modern pilgrims can combine the speed of a cycle with no little effort, and so arrive, full of virtue, at Compostela.

This road from Le Puy travels south and west to the Pyrénées, cutting across the grain of the country, up and down a series of great river valleys, across the Loire, the Allier, the Truyère, the Lot, the Tarn, up and down, endlessly. Needing all the help I could get, I chose a good bicycle, and I have it before me as I write, a black, ten-speed tourer by F.W. Evans of The Cut, London SE1, still dusty from the Road. I remember forcing it up the steep road to Roncesvalles and soaring on it down the rough track from the hospice at Cebrero. Certainly it made me sweat, but sweat makes the true pilgrim, something far more than a mere tourist, a far cry from those unlucky souls who swept past me in their air-conditioned coaches, or landed directly at Lavacola by jet, missing all that the true pilgrim finds on this glorious journey down the old Road.

The bicycle is a good steed for the modern pilgrim. Indeed, had they existed at the time, I suspect that our medieval forebears would have adopted them with alacrity. I do not intend to go into the technical side of cycle-touring in any detail. All you need to know lies in other books, or in the appendices. I would only stress that the real flavour of the Road comes from making the 'true pilgrimage' and that means travelling on foot or by horse or cycle.

Cruising along at an average of fifty miles a day, my cycle got me to Compostela within the month, and the cathedral authorities at Compostela recognise cycling as the mark and method of true pilgrims and will grant them their *compostelles*, as a sign of someone who has completed the 'true pilgrimage of St James'.

Although William Langland said, 'A pilgrim has leave to lie all his life hereafter,' I might conclude this introduction to St James with a personal declaration. It is facile to pretend that anyone takes the Road to Santiago simply to go on a journey; there is always another reason, and it always slips out in the end. In my case I went to get away from a life that seemed increasingly sterile, in which I could not find a reason to be happy. I left for Compostela because I had slowly but completely run out of the ability to tolerate my life as it was. The world seemed to have run dry and lost its colour. Living in it had become a pointless exercise. I suppose I was simply depressed. The Road seemed to offer a little chink of light, and I got up wearily and followed it. Like Montaigne, 'I knew well what I fled from but not for what I seek.'

I cannot think that I am alone in all this; everyone I met on the journey had a reason for the Road — to forget a death or a divorce, to remake a friendship, to make one last effort to befriend a growing child, or simply to rediscover that something in oneself that makes life, LIFE.

Chapter 1
The Road to Aubrac

'Remove not the landmarks which thy fathers have set'

Proverbs

So, let us begin this journey down the Pilgrim Road. See me, on this warm summer morning, at the station of Le Puy in the Velay, unwrapping my cycle from the protective cardboard cocoon so thoughtfully provided by French Rail at Lyon. All my luggage is in two Karrimor panniers and a handlebar bag, as on other trips, but I do carry one essential extra most necessary for the pilgrim. On the handlebar bag is suspended a cockle-shell, the *coquille de St Jacques,* the symbol of the Compostela traveller. I have also sewn on a badge of my arms, the owls and lily on the sable field, in the hope that other historically-minded travellers will come over to enquire. I feel nervous, but the usual tasks of putting the bike together and fitting the panniers remind me that all journeys have their beginnings and all will be well once I actually get going. That done, there is nothing left but to chain the cycle to the railings and cross the road to the *Hotel Licorn* for lunch with the lady from the Tourist Office and hear about the city of Le Puy, one of the great assembly points for pilgrims on the Road to Compostela.

*   *   *

Le Puy is a curious city. It lies in the green country of the Velay, and is set on a loop in the Loire. It has been a starting point on the Road to Compostela for centuries and indeed, the first recorded pilgrim to Compostela was Gottshalk, Bishop of Le Puy, who went to Santiago in AD951. Le Puy is a good place to start such a journey, for it is a pilgrim city in its

*St Michel
d'Aiguille,
Le Puy*

own right, with the shrine of a Black Virgin, Notre Dame de Puy, in the great dark cathedral. That apart, even on first sight it is an unusual city, dominated by jagged spikes of volcanic rock. One of these is occupied by the minute chapel of St Michel d'Aiguille, St Michael of the Needle, and the other, the Rocher Corneille, by a huge red statue of the Virgin, Notre Dame de France, erected in 1860 and forged from the metal of 213 cannon captured from the Russians during the Crimean War at the taking of Sebastapol. It looks. . . hideous.

Over lunch, Martine Granouillet, the tourism lady, mapped out my instant pilgrim programme, a process interspeded with groans as we tried by turns to lift the wine bottle from the ice bucket and failed, defeated by our common affliction, tennis elbow. I felt this ailment to be particularly unfair as I don't even play tennis.

Pilgrims have always had rituals to perform before the start of the journey. It has never been easy to get away from the daily task, particularly in medieval times when hands were precious. Permission had to be obtained from the local lord or bishop, and this permission was usually limited to a specific period of time, and depended on the declared destination. Priests bound for Jerusalem usually received their full stipend for up to three years, but laymen were usually expected to return before the harvest, or in time to perform their feudal obligations. In addition, there were social responsibilities. In 1406 a preacher wrote that: '. . . a pilgrim must first pay his debts, set his house in order, take leave of his neighbours, and so go forth.'

Pilgrims had their own distinctive garb, consisting of *sclavine,* a long homespun tunic, a *scip* or wallet, a gourd or waterbottle, and a long staff, an outfit well described by Sir Walter Raleigh:

'Give me my scallop shell of quiet
My staff of faith to walk upon
My scrip of Joy, eternal diet
My bottle of salvation,
My gown of glory, hope's true gage
And then I'll take my pilgrimage.

Like me, the pilgrim to St James often carried a scallop-shell, supposedly the symbol of St James. As I soon discovered in my role as a true pilgrim, the scallop-shell is a useful item in its own right. Mine served as a plate, a cup, and a shaving dish, most useful for scooping a trickle of water from a half-dry ditch, though unlike the medieval pilgrim, I had no need to use it as a begging bowl. That apart, my cycling rig of shorts, trainers and tee-shirt was neither romantic nor traditional.

Apart from the nobility, few pilgrims carried much money, although many were sponsored by their neighbours. All relied on alms or food being provided by monasteries and hospices along the way, although those who could afford it were expected to make a donation in return, and pilgrim fare, at best, was hardly nourishing. Any pilgrim knew at the start that the journey involved deprivation. On the morning of

25

departure, the pilgrim would lay his staff and scrip upon the altar of his parish church and attend a service. Then, accompanied by wellwishers and those of the local pilgrim confraternity, he would set out upon his journey, and our day in Le Puy followed a similar pattern.

I have a very low boredom threshold, and in anticipation of many church visits on the way, restricted our tour of Le Puy to just three, rather different, foundations. The climb up to the Chapel of St Michel is a leg-testing 268 uneven steps, but the views and the chapel are worth it. St Michel's is really a miniature church with a nave and a tower, quite exquisite, and one of the finest of those pillar churches in France and dedicated to the archangel. It was interesting to note, even here, Mozarabic influences on the slightly curved doors and windows. Descending from St Michel we went on to the Cathedral of Notre Dame, diverting into St Laurent Church which contains some of the much divided remains of my hero, Bertrand du Guesclin, sometime Constable of France, who thrashed the English during the Hundred Year's War. St Denis in Paris has Bertrand's body, St Sauver in Brittany his heart, but St Laurent lays claim to his entrails, which rest under a tomb in the choir.

The Cathedral of Notre-Dame-de-Puy is a vast, dark, rambling, fortified place reached up a long flight of steps into a porch where beggars crouch in the shadows. In medieval times Le Puy was a pilgrim centre in its own right, containing one of the rare Auvergne Black Virgins, supposedly brought from the Holy Land after the First Crusade. The original was burned during the Revolution, but a replica, suitably dusky and clad in rich garments, now stands on the High Altar. Pilgrims would gather here before descending the steps into the rue des Pelerins to the rue de Compostela. Before leaving, the Rector produced the *Livre de Pelerins,* which is signed by all departing pilgrims, and invited me to add my name. A steady stream of names and dates slid down the page, mostly French, some Germans, no English. A lady from Lyon, also on a bicycle, had departed from Le Puy four days before, *'pour voir Monsieur St Jacques'.*

Next morning the great cathedral bell tolled across empty

rain-slick streets, as I wheeled my bike down the steep cobbles from the church porch; the light was grey and flat, the streets still and empty. It seemed the perfect moment to depart.

*　　*　　*

The road to Aubrac, the first stage on my journey, climbs steeply from Le Puy, and I would like to state that I rode up to the crest without stopping, if not without puffing. This road is now a tourist route, called the *Route de la Bête du Gevaudan,* in memory of the fabulous *Bête,* a wolf or werewolf, which terrorised the countryside hereabouts at the end of the eighteenth century until it was shot by the King's Huntsman, who despatched it with a silver bullet. I was too busy looking hopefully about for other pilgrims, or some sign of their

27

passing, to worry about ancient werewolves and passed on quickly to Bains, over pleasant rolling country at around 1,000m mark, to the pretty town of St Privat, set high above the great gorge of my first river, the Allier. This road is flanked for much of the way by the GR65 footpath, *Le Chemin de St Jacques de Compostelle,* one of the longest in the network of the *Grande Randonnée.* Both road and footpath were empty on this Monistrol d'Allier, past the pilgrim chapel at Rochegude and my first stop at the *Hotel Sarda,* run by an Anglo-French couple, David and Jöelle West who, like the rector in Le Puy, keep a book for the pilgrim traveller.

'We don't see many, but then they don't all stop,' explained Jöelle. 'We get most of our trade locally, from the Auvergnats. I think they like David's English sense of humour — and the Royal Family,' she added thoughtfully. 'The locals are fascinated by the Royals.' Apart from being notably dour, the Auvergnats, the people of the Auvergne who are, by tradition, the providers of barmen to Paris, are lovers of good food. 'A group will come in with, say, Fr3,000 to spend, and ask, "What sort of meal can you do?" Well, for that we can do

Rue des Pelerins, Le Puy

a lot. All the spare cash hereabouts goes on food . . . but we would like to see more English.'

The absence of the English is not too surprising, for there are many roads to Compostela. In the Middle Ages, the jounrey to St James was extremely popular with English pilgrims. Samuel Purchas, who wrote around 1417, though describing an earlier journey, opens his account with the words, 'Here beginneth the Way, that is marked and made with Montjoies, from the Land of England unto Saint Jamez in Galis, and from thenze to Rome and thenze to Jerusalem, and so again unto England. . . .' *Purchas His Pilgrimes* was published in book form in 1635, a century after the breach with Rome had virtually extinguished the English pilgrimage. Many great or famous English nobles and clerics went to Compostela: St Godric of Norfolk went there several times between 1102 and 1170; John of Gaunt, brother of the Black Prince, was actually married at Santiago and from there claimed the throne of Castile; a Scots lord Sir James Douglas passed through Compostela and died fighting the Moors in Spain when bearing the heart of Robert the Bruce to the Holy Land; Margery Kempe from Kings Lynn went via Bristol in 1426; William Way of Eton College went by sea to St James, landing at Coruña in 1456; Earl Rivers passed by Santiago in 1477, to serve in the Spanish wars as did his contemporary Lord Scales, who was wounded at the siege of Loja; Henry VI

St Privat

issued 918 licenses to merchant captains in 1428, permitting the transport of pilgrims, and 2,500 personal passports were issued in 1434, which was a Holy Year, when the feast of St James falls on a Sunday.

Men may leve all gaymes
That sayln to Saint Jamys.

— sang a ballad in the time of Henry VI, and the voyage to Coruña was certainly no less dangerous than the journey overland, but many pilgrims reported seeing numerous English ships in the harbour there, bringing pilgrims and returning with cargoes of Spanish wine and bow-staves.

Apart from the famous, there were many simple, unrecorded folk, who scraped up the money and the energy to undertake this perilous pilgrimage. Andrew Boorde, a doctor, made one of the last medieval pilgrimages in about 1538, and returned bearing his *compostelle* and 'a powerful physick'. Boorde went overland and wrote on his return: 'I do assure all that world that I had rather go five times out of Englande to Rome than one to Compostelle; by water it is no payne but by land it is the greatest journey that an Englishman may go.'

The strength of the cult of St James in England also appears in the number of English churches dedicated to St James the Greater, 414 according to the ecclesiastical authority, Francis Bond. Some of these, like St James Garlickhythe in the City of London, were assembly points for pilgrims, and bore the emblem of St James. The greatest English foundation dedicated to St James was Reading Abbey, which was run by the Cluniacs and contained, as a very rare relic, the hand of St James, cut off at his execution, when he raised it to ward off the fatal blow. The Empress Matilda, wife of Geoffrey Plantagenet and daughter of Henry I, obtained this relic when she went to Santiago in 1125. She gave it to her father who placed it in his newly-founded abbey at Reading, where he himself was later buried. Pilgrims heading for Southampton passed by Reading and the abbey enjoyed considerable popularity and prosperity until it was destroyed in 1539, and Hugh Farringdon, the last abbot, hanged at his own gate at the orders of Henry VIII.

The hand disappeared during the Reformation, but in the last century, when workmen were dismantling one of the crumbling walls, they found a mummified hand concealed near the High Altar. This is believed to be the hand of St James and it now rests, small, dark and shrivelled, in the care of the Catholic Church of St Peter, at Marlow-on-Thames. Accord-ing to legend, St James made himself felt from time to time in Reading. When a knight came to beg his assistance for a broken arm that refused to heal, St James helped him, but when the arm was healed and the knight then refused to give alms in gratitude, the saint broke his other arm; or so it is said. Reading Abbey is a ruined shell today, a pale relic of the pilgrimage.

*   *   *

The Sarda is a nice hotel and I would have liked to stay longer and sample some of that well-flavoured cooking, but big meals in the middle of the day play havoc with a cyclist's

The martyrdom of Hugh Faringdon, last Abbot of Reading,
November 15, 1539, from a painting in Reading Art Gallery

31

Guidestone on the pilgrims' road near Sauges

stamina. I had to press on, over the high mountains of the Margaride, up another of those long, winding ascents from the Allier, still in the saddle and blessing those low gears, a steep 7km to La Vachellerie and on to the little town of Sauges, the Porte du Gevaudan, glowing in the heat of the mid-day sun. Sauges has a large church, which contains the relics of St Benilde, but already I fear to weary you with churches on this journey; I prefer castles and paid more attention to the great tower which overlooks the town, the *Tour des Anglais,* held by the English during the Hundred Years' War and used as a base for harrying the Gevaudan. If the French really do not like the English, of which I remain doubtful, they do have good cause. The sun was up, so I had lunch here in one of those little places where the lone waitress takes your order in silence, and then shrieks it out embarrassingly to the chef as she elbows her way through the kitchen door.

After Sauges the Road turns south, rising and falling, but less steeply now, to Esplantas and Chanalailles and up to the pilgrim chapel of St Roch on the crest of the Margaride. St

Sauges

Roch appears regularly on the Road, dressed as a Compostela pilgrim, but then it is St Roch and not St James who is the patron saint of pilgrims. St Roch is usually portrayed standing, leaning on his staff and pointing coyly at his thigh, and is often accompanied by a dog, bearing a loaf of bread in his mouth. A holy man, he developed a chancre in his groin, so he retired to a wood where his faithful hound brought him food. This pilgrim chapel marks the boundary between the *départements* of Haute Loire and Lozère. There is a small shelter here for pilgrims, and a spring of cold water, most handy for those who, like me, arrive on the crest with empty waterbottles. From here the Road descends swiftly, swinging down the mountainside to St-Alban-sur-Limagnole in a series of long curves. St Alban is a pretty town with an attractive Romanesque church dedicated to England's proto-martyr, but I did not linger. By now I was beginning to feel distinctly tired, and there was still a good distance to cover, walking over yet another hill, then riding down to Pont

The pilgrim chapel of St Roch, Margaride

des Estrets and the infant river Truyère. Then up again, slow and weary under the evening sun, before a long run downhill took me to my first night-stop at Aumont on the edge of the Aubrac plateau, seventy miles from my start at Le Puy, too much for the first day on a hard saddle, but still many miles indeed from Compostela.

St-Alban-sur-Limagnole

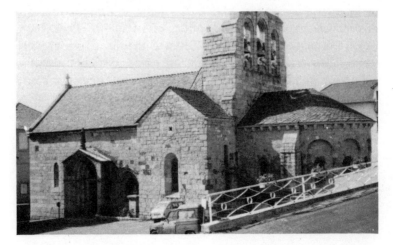

Chapter 2
The Road to Conques

'The holy blisful martyr for to seke
That them hath hopen when that were sick.'

Chaucer: Prologue — The Canterbury Tales

Over the years I have stayed several times in the Grand Hotel
de la Gare at Aumont and always arrive there in a mess. The
Aubrac plateau is a rugged place, perfect for summer walking
and winter ski touring, and after a week out there in the wild, I
like to descend on the Grand Hotel for a much needed spot of
comfort. The proprietors, the *famille* Prouhèze, aim to cater
for the carriage trade and are justly proud of their Michelin
rosette, but accept the periodic arrival of a scruffy, unshaven
English wreck with a commendable resignation. I fell on to a
chair by the porch, viewed with alarm by the other, more
elegant patrons, and cried loudly for beer and *Orangina*. Two
hours, a bottle of Macon and a dish of *Escalopes de truites aux
oignons, comfits a l'écorce d'oranges* later, I was almost myself
again, and practically cheerful.

From Aumont the Road runs south and west across the
Aubrac. The Michelin guidebook describes the Aubrac as
'mountainous', since it runs at the 1000m mark, but it is really
rather more a vast plateau of small rolling hills, forested to
the east and west, open and windswept in the centre. In winter
the Aubrac can be a fearsome place, under snow for many
months of the year, and I heard later that when another
English pilgrim, Peter Johnson, passed this way some weeks
before me, in the second week of June, he had been met with a
blizzard and deep snow, in the second week,

Today, though, the Aubrac was delightful. A carpet of
flowers dotted with browsing cows spread out on either hand,
a clear blue sky above, and the Road ahead lay empty of
traffic and sparkling in the sunshine. The little pilgrim chapel
set beside the Road at Lasbros was already open, the candles

Circus animals at Nasbinals

lit, flickering in the gloom, and walkers appeared ahead on the GR65. After Quatre Chemins the countryside opened out, and at Malbuzion I turned off for Rieutort, a half-abandoned village, littered with large granite drinking troughs, known as *abreuvoirs,* then past the waterfall at Deroc and back on the main road to Nasbinals.

Nasbinals has a fine Romanesque church and the town blazon bears the scallop-shell symbol of St James, but there is precious little else to stir the pilgrim. The circus was in town this Sunday morning, adding a little colour to the scene; a camel tied to a tree in the square and a llama browsing contentedly on a traffic island helped to disconcert a number of motorists. One thing Nasbinals does offer is good views over the Southern Auvernge, for the road out climbs up to 1,324m and reveals the hills of Cantal to the north, the mountains of the Margeride I had crossed the day before and to the south, Mont Lozère and the distant blue hills of the Cévennes.

And so to Aubrac. Aubrac is just a little place today but it has always been a major stop on the pilgrim road, one of those 'places of obligation' which all true pilgrims must visit. In

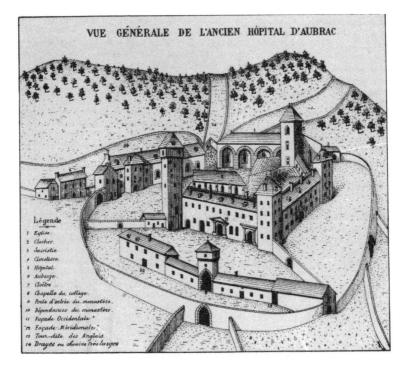

VUE GÉNÉRALE DE L'ANCIEN HÔPITAL D'AUBRAC

Légende
1 Eglise.
2 Clocher.
3 Sacristie.
4 Cimetière.
5 Hôpital.
6 Auberge.
7 Cloître.
8 Chapelle du collège.
9 Porte d'entrée du monastère.
10 Dépendances du monastère.
11 Façade Occidentale.
12 Façade Méridionale.
13 Tour dite des Anglais.
14 Drayes ou chemins très larges.

An early view of the hospice at Aubrac

1120, a Flemish knight, Adalard, was returning from
Compostela when he was caught on the Aubrac by a sudden
storm and nearly perished. He founded and endowed the
hospice at Aubrac, and having garrisoned it with twelve
soldier monks, charged them with the task of escorting
pilgrims across the Aubrac and protecting them from
robbery. A great bell, *Maria,* was hung in the church of Notre-
Dame-des-Pauvres and tolled at nightfall in fog or bad
weather to guide any wandering pilgrim to safety. For
centuries there after, and especially during the Hundred
Years' War, when the English Free-Companies preyed upon
the pilgrim trade, Aubrac was a place of safety, and it still
looks a snug place today, tucked into the hills across the
valley with the old track to Compostela leading across the
fields towards the church. 'The way of St James in fine but
narrow, as narrow as the path of Salvation', and so it is here,

37

*Tour des
Anglais,
Aubrac*

on any dark night or stormy day.

The village thrives today as a walking and cross-country skiing centre, with several hotels, all dominated by the major fortification, a tall tower, the *Tour des Anglais*, now a *gite d'etape* for pilgrims, and the Church of Our Lady, a vast, damp place with a notice on the wall telling how Adalard established this hospice, *'en loco horroris et vastes solitudinis'*. A pilgrim book of a table by the altar tells the story of St James and the *Livre d'Or* invites your signature. I saw that I had already gained a day on the lady from Lyon.

Groups of walkers sat at tables in the sunshine outside the Hotel Moderne or were lunching on the local Auvergnat speciality, *aligote,* a cheese and potato stew, at Chez Germaine, a great pilgrim hangout. 'Are you going to St Jacques?' I asked, noticing the scallop-shells dangling from their rucksacks. 'No, no, not this time, only to Conques. Have you been to Conques? Conques is wonderful, a *merveille.* You must go to Conques.' So I bade them goodbye and set out for Conques.

After Aubrac the Road and the scenery change. The Road

descends into the valley of Lot, which is called the Olt hereabouts in the local patois. It is a long, steep descent, trying to avoid a spill, treadling the brakes to stop the wheelrims from overheating on a swift five-mile run to St Chély d'Aubrac, which seemed a good spot for lunch. Cheese and fruit from the shop in the main street, water scooped from the river in my scallop-shell, and a delightful picnic by the old bridge across the river which bears a cross carved with the figure of a Compostela pilgrim. This bridge lies on the old, old pilgrim track — centuries old. From St Chély the Road climbs up to the crest by La Remise, a slow walk on this scorching hot afternoon, rewarded by a long easy descent into the old town of St Côme.

St Côme used to be fortified and there are still relics of the old walls and castle in the central parts round the church, which has a curiously twisted steeple. On this afternoon, St Côme slumbered in the sun. Nothing moved except a group of lads plastering a car with paper flowers for a wedding and the occasional dog panting slowly from one patch of shade to another.

From St Côme the Road leads west, along the right bank of the Lot to Espalion and Estaing, two pretty riverside towns. Espalion is the larger, dominated by the ruins of a medieval *château-fort,* once the seat of the Lords of Calmont. There is an old bridge here, one of several along the Lot built by that curious order, the *Frères Pontiff,* monks who served God and his pilgrims by building bridges, a most useful and skilful task. At Espalion, apart from the riverside views, there is the redstone eleventh-century Church of Perse in the town centre, and the little Romanesque Chapel of St-Pierre-de-Bessuejouls set by the river, but I was beginning to weary in the heat of the day and pressed on to Estaing.

Estaing is a splendid spot, with a well-preserved castle, yet another medieval bridge and a maze of narrow streets and small bridges among the old houses of the town. I dumped my kit in the Aux Armes d'Estaing, chained up my bicycle in the garage and set off to explore. The Estaings, who had their seat here, were a military family, and implacable foes of the English. Dieudonné d'Estaing won great glory at the battle of Bovines in 1214, the battle which finally expelled King John

St Chély d'Aubrac

from his Duchy of Normandy, and was allowed to add the Royal lilies to the family arms. As soldiers or prelates they played a prominent part in French society until the end of the eighteenth century, when Charles-Hector, the then Comte d'Estaing, a noted seaman who had played havoc with English shipping on the trade routes to India, fell foul of the Revolutionaries and was promptly executed. 'Send my head to the English,' he told the crowd before the scaffold, 'they will pay you well for it.'

Today the great castle of the lords of Estaing is home to a religious community, but they allow the public in to climb the stairs to the walls, from which there are fine views along the valley and to the old Gothic bridge which carries the statue of François d'Estaing, Bishop and Count of Rodez, who lived here from 1460 to 1529. I like Estaing, a sleepy little town, still sunk in the Middle Ages. On the way in, pedalling through the heat beside the river, I had dreamed of dinner, *truite aux amandes* perhaps, with a nice bottle of *Perle* from the vineyards of Gaillac, and when I sat down at my table that evening, both were listed on the menu — perfect.

Castle and medieval bridge, Estaing

After my regular evening worry over the map I left Estaing early the following morning, in the chill just after dawn, and the day began deceptively easily with the Road continuing along the river, through the jagged gorges of the Lot towards Entraygues, a nice, level, seductive route. After 10km though, the Compostela path crosses the river and begins to climb the side of a gorge to Golinhac, 6km slog up an endless series of curves. I tottered into Golinhac halfway through the morning when the sun was already blasting from the sky, and fell into a café for the first of many *Oranginas* — the cyclist's salvation. The snag here is that Golinhac is not at the top of the climb; it is a deception. The Road climbs again, past another chapel Notre-Dame-des-Hauteurs, our well-named Lady of the Heights, travels briefly along the crest and then falls away steeply into the equally well-named valley of the Daze at Espeyrac, and yet another long climb up again to Senergues. This set the pattern for the next few days;

punishing heat, steep climbs, a short run along the summit of the ridge, a rapid descent, and then the mixture as before. This can be wearying but the traveller, not knowing what lies ahead, travels hopefully. The winds set hard against me, booming in hot as a furnace from the west, but the effort was worth it.

After what seemed like ages the road fell away for the last time that day and swept me down into the hilltown and pilgrim centre of Conques, in the green heart of the Rouergue.

*   *   *

Conques is a good place to discuss the cult of relics for, set in these remote hills, Conques owes its entire fame to the possession of one relic, that of Ste Foy, and it came by that through theft. Belief in the effectiveness of relics, either to work miracles or purge guilt, seems to have existed from the earliest times, and *brandea,* the relics of holy men, were soon much sought after by religious foundations, mainly because of faith but also because they were profitable. The best kind of relic would be the actual body of the saint, as at Compostela or Canterbury, but provided there was some connection, even rocks or dust would do. Parts of the body were almost efficacious as the complete item and this gave rise to dismemberment and the sharing of relics, as well as to some rather unfortunate or comic incidents.

The tale is told of an abbey, already doing rather well from possessing the arms of St Ann, which decided to invest some of the profits in further attractions. They sent one of their monks off with a bag of gold to see what he could find and he returned triumphant after several months to reveal his find to the assembled chapter — the third arm of St Ann!

Another pilgrim pointed out to a monk that he had already been shown the head of John the Baptist at another abbey nearby, but the monk blandly stated that the other relic was the head of the saint 'as a young man', while theirs dated from the time when St John was old and full of wisdom. Other relics might include such surprises as the Virgin's milk, a vial of Christ's breath, the tip of Satan's tail, tears shed on the Cross. The list is endless, often spurious and the cult of relics was clearly open to abuse. There are said to be enough pieces of the True Cross about to build Noah another Ark, but in an age when men could combine piety with practicality, the cult prospered, to the benefit of pilgrim souls and the great advantage of the Church.

Behind the cult of relics lay the theory of the Treasury of Mercy laid up by Christ and the Saints. Holy men had virtue to spare and so they had, in effect, opened up an investment account in Heaven on which repentant sinners could draw if they made some effort to show contrition. Going on a pilgrimage was a suitable gesture which gained indulgence. This pilgrimage to St James, for example, if made as a true pilgrim, gains the remission of half the time in Purgatory, a great comfort to those of us who do it twice. An indulgence remits the penance, not the guilt, and there were two forms of indulgence, the Plenary, which could remit all the penance due on the sins of life to date, and the Partial, which remitted only a portion. As the medieval Church decayed, pardoners increasingly sold indulgences, one of the abuses which infuriated Luther and sparked the Reformation, but it was not always so. A careful pilgrim could notch up indulgences as he went from shrine to shrine, a day here, a year there, every little helps when hellfire is the option. An indulgence was the usual reward for the completion of a long, arduous pilgrimage, but a pilgrimage needed an object of veneration, and here Conques had a problem. The great abbey at Conques was a Cluniac foundation, lying on the Compostela Road, and it attracted thousands of pilgrims who had to be fed, but who then passed on to make their donations and offerings at two other nearby shrines, Rocamadour or Agen; Conques, *sans* relic, got nothing and something had to be done.

The abbot summoned one of his brethren, the monk Aronisdus, and sent him off in secular garments to join the community at Agen, which was doing very nicely from the relics of Ste Foy, a Christian maiden martyred by Diocletian.

Aronisdus was duly accepted at Agen and waited ten years before his turn came to guard their precious relic. Then he was over the wall one dark night and back to Conques as fast as his sandals would carry him. Legend has it that Ste Foy herself conjured up the mist which hid him from his outraged pursuers. Robbed of the relic, the pilgrim stream swerved past Agen and Conques prospered.

Needless to say, there was an outcry, but once the relics of Ste Foy were installed at Conques, they fell under the powerful protection of Cluny, which paid compensation to Agen but flatly refused to return them. Anyway, there was nothing new in stealing relics to endow an abbey on the pilgrim road. The abbey at Vézelay owed its position at the head of the Burgundy road to the possesssion of relics of Ste Mary Magdalen, which the monks of St Maximum in Provence had sent to Vézelay for safe-keeping. The monks of Vézelay refused to return them, for good relics were profitable, especially if they could, from time to time, produce a miracle by way of promotion.

One of the fascinations of the medieval world is that, now it is gone, we can see it, if not clearly, then at least in the round. Medieval man was pragmatic and although that era has become shrouded with legends of saintliness and chivalry, there were usually practical, economic or political reasons for what he did, as much in the Church as in the political or commercial sphere. No monastic order began with the aim of profit. Most orders were a reaction against the worldliness of the parent community, but though a monk could not acquire wealth, his order or community could, and when intelligent men band together to work, even for the glory of God, the venture is frequently profitable. The Order of Cluny was founded in Burgundy in AD910. The monks were Benedictines, following the Rule established by St Benedict at Monte Cassino, which was, and indeed still is, the blueprint for monastic communities. By the year 1100 Cluny had over 2,000 daughter houses and over 10,000 monks, spread all over Christendom. Cluny was in many respects a great university, famed and respected for the learning of the monks and supported by many Christian kings, notably those hard-pressed sovereigns of Spain, who needed the pilgrim road and the Cluniac hospices to pump men, arms and money into their often beleaguered kingdoms.

The Mother House at Cluny was destroyed by the mob during the Revolution, an act of vandalism that appalled Napoleon.

Levell, levell with the ground
These towers do lye,
Which with their glittering tops
Pierced once the skye.

The Cluniacs have gone but many of their houses remain, splendidly preserved, along the Road to Compostela. The monks of Cluny ran the pilgrim traffic to Compostela as a business and they saw to it that any investment in relics paid off in practical terms, and as far as Conques is concerned still does. Baking in the sunshine, the golden walls of Conques echoed to the sound of voices, the echo of the organ playing softly in the cathedral and everywhere the jangle of tills.

Ste Foy was martyred in AD303 and her relics were purloined from Agen in the ninth century, after which the rapid growth in pilgrim traffic necessitated a new church. The present building dates from the eleventh century, and to my gradually adjusting eye, was instantly recognisable as a pilgrim church. The building is pure Romanesque and the west door, approached across a cobbled square, bears a splendidly-carved tympanum, a masterpiece showing the Last Judgement and the dire fate awaiting unrepentant sinners. Enter under the pipes of that now-thundering organ and the interior is vast, the floor sloping towards the door, another pilgrim feature, so that the mud carried in by the pilgrim feet could be washed away easily. Wide aisles or ambulatories circle the nave and choir so that pilgrims could file past the relics of Ste Foy, which would be kept by the High Altar, and then round past the offertory box and out again. It was all swift, very efficient, and as one might expect from the Cluniacs, well organised.

Ste Foy was believed to be interested in the fate of prisoners taken in the Spanish Wars and many pilgrims to Conques came to request her intercession on behalf of relatives held

Reliquary of Ste Foy, Conques

captive by the Moors. On their release the former captives brought their chains to Ste Foy, and the beautiful wrought-iron altar screen which envelops the choir is said to be forged from fetters.

The curious and far from attractive reliquary of the saint is kept in the abbey treasury in the cloisters, among what is probably the finest remaining medieval church treasury in Europe. Apart from Ste Foy's reliquary, *La Majesté de Ste Foy'*, a rather squat, pop-eyed statue covered with goldleaf and studded with jewels, there are reliquaries donated by Pepin of Aquitaine in the ninth century and one of the rare 'alphabet' reliquaries, said to have been given by Charlemagne to all his favourite monasteries. Conques, being the most favoured foundation, got the letter 'A'. There are church treasures here from the ninth to sixteenth centuries, and all might have been lost at the Revolution but for the prompt action of the mayor. Hearing that the mob from Rodez was marching on his town, aiming to sack the church, he distributed the treasure among the townspeople, telling them to hide it carefully. Many items were walled up in houses and stayed hidden for years before they were recovered; indeed, some say that the walls of Conques still contain items from this famous and most splendid medieval treasury.

Conques is a pretty, gem-like little town, very medieval and an essential stop on the pilgrim road. The pilgrims still flow through on foot or bike, and the local people are used to them. I left my bike and baggage near the coach park, protected by my scallop-shell, and wandered about the town, up the Rue de St Jacques, which leads into the town, and down to the little Chapel of St Roch, patron of pilgrims, which overlooks the valley of the Ouche. It was still terribly hot and when I saw a thermometer registering 37 °C (99 °F) in the shade, I decided to stay off the road for the rest of the day and award myself some more luxury in the Hotel Ste Foy just opposite the abbey, and spent the afternoon down by the pilgrim bridge, paddling about contentedly in the river, feeling myself relax as I slipped into the mood of the pilgrimage.

As dusk fell, the tourists departed. I wandered out again after dinner to walk about the quiet streets, past walls still warm from the afternoon sun. Deep purple shadows fell across the cobblestone, as a huge white moon hoisted itself up above the surrounding hills and spread its light across the town. Conques sighed and fell asleep.

Chapter 3
The Road to Moissac

'Forth pilgrim, forth: Forth Beste, out of thy
stal,
Know thy countree, look up, thank God of al;
Hold thy way clere, and let thy ghost thee lede.'

Chaucer: Balade de Bon Conseyle

I must get on. *'Ultreia',* as the pilgrims cry. I should have left
Conques early in the day, but I lingered, to take another walk
around the quiet morning streets and sit again in the coolness
of the abbey. After three days storming across the hot hills
and valleys, I felt like a rest. Someone played the organ again,
softly this time, a bell tolled from time to time but no one
came to the morning service. Conques came gradually to life
in the streets outside, shutters came down, tables appeared
before the cafés, and the first coach groaned into the parking
area; it was time to go.

Conques is divided into two parts, the old town hugging
closely around the abbey on the hill, and the slightly more
modern *bourg* down by the river, where another humpbacked
bridge leads across the sparkling river to the far wall of the
gorge. Within five minutes I had to get off the bike and my
long calvary commenced which lasted for the next few days. I
discovered, not for the last time, that of all the terrors facing
the cycle-tourist of a certain age heading for Compostela,
heat was by far the worst. Keep cool and I could climb any hill
and cover my daily distance with ease. Well, perhaps not with
ease.

As the temperature rose though, trouble began, and when
compounded by steep hills, a rough gravel road surface
which sucks at the tyres, and loaded panniers, the Road to
Compostela became a calvary indeed — and so it was on the
climb from Conques to Noailhac. The sun was already high
across the valley and it pinned me to the rock wall like a fly. I

began to proceed in short spurts, hurrying from one inadequate patch of shade to the next, pushing the ever-heavier bicycle, toe-clips clanging in the road, dripping with sweat, gasping. By the time I was halfway up the hill I had drained my waterbottle and the sun had scorched the skin on my back and legs. This is one of the problems with the Road; it cannot be difficult. This is well-populated Europe, not a journey across desolation, so all you have to do is stop and that is the constant temptation, so 'Get thee behind me Satan, and *push*'.

I resolved to leave before dawn in future, and pay more attention to the weather reports. So it went on, for nearly two hours until the road finally levelled out and I tottered into the deeper shade of a small copse and lay down for a rest by yet another Chapel of St Roch. It was some time before I took much interest in my surroundings. The footpath to St Roch from Noailhac is marked with crosses, and lies on the GR65. It is a quiet, evocative spot and the chapel shelters one of those familiar statues of St Roch, dressed here, in pilgrim garb, the shoulders of his cloak and the front of his hat bearing the scallop-shell of St James, a now familiar sight of this pilgrimage. It seems a slight connection with St James, but the ecclesiastical authorities in Compostela were quick to adopt the scallop-shell as their particular symbol, and controlled the sale of scallop-shell badges in shops in the town, yet another source of revenue from the pilgrim trade.

Dante defined three kinds of pilgrim; those who went to Jerusalem and brought back a palm leaf as a sign of their accomplishment, for which reason they were called *palmers;* those who went to Rome and were called *roamers;* and those who went to Compostela and were the true pilgrims. It was never that clear-cut, however. The scallop-shell quickly became *the* pilgrim symbol and was adopted, for example by the abbey at Mont-St-Michel in Normandy, which sells scallop-shell badges bearing the arms of St Michael to this very day, while all travellers to any shrine were pilgrims. One of the practical benefits of making a true pilgrimage was my discovery that the dish-shaped scallop-shell is useful; which, far more than legend or symbolism, probably accounted for its popularity. Besides, even as a symbol, it predates Christianity; the Romans used it as a symbol of Venus, and it had a secular use as well, in heraldry. Some twenty of the old families of England bear the scallop-shell as a charge on their arms, and Boutell, the heraldic authority, writes that it is 'the mark of the pilgrim in olden times and held in high esteem by heralds', but here again, some other authorities state that it has no pilgrim relevance but indicates instead some maritime or nautical connection.

The scallop-shell is often, incorrectly, referred to as a cockleshell, and pilgrims vowing to make the journey to St James were said to have 'taken the cockle'; even oysters became involved, for St James' Day, 25 July, marked the start of the oyster-eating season, when the children built little grottoes from the shells, and begged for money in the streets crying 'A penny for the grotto'.

Whoever, or whatever other claims there may be, the scallop-shell is chiefly noted as the symbol of those who make the pilgrimage to Santiago. They are still sold in shops and stalls around the Cathedral and most pilgrims acquire one before setting out their journey, carrying it proudly and cherishing it thereafter. Bearing the scallop-shell could gain the pilgrim freedom from tolls and ensure the protection of the Church. Scallop-shells have been found in graves, showing the pilgrim's last earthly journey. I am proud of mine, and it hangs now in my study, waiting on other journeys to St James.

Back in the hills above Conques, peering through the doorway of the chapel at the pilgrim-garbed St Roch, my main thought was that St James might have got himself martyred at some more temperate time of the year and so spared his followers a journey across Europe in the hottest months of summer. Not that it would have made much difference. Thomas à Becket was martyred in December, an inconvenient time for travellers in England, so his saint's day was changed to July, the date when his relics were translated to the high altar.

From Noailhac the Road runs west along the open ridge and descends steeply into the town of Decazeville, a mining and industrial centre, and somewhat short on charm. Everyone had sensibly taken shelter from the heat and I joined the crowd in one of the darker cafés to drink more *Orangina* and watch the Wimbledon tennis matches on the television set high in the corner, leaping back into the present from my journey through the past. Here I lurked, while the sun smote the streets, only venturing out late in the afternoon to ride down the Lot valley towards that night's halt in the town of Figeac. Fate has a way of catching one out, for this road is open and the heat from the road surface was tremendous. At Capdenac the road swerves up the hill, and following it through a tunnel I found myself facing another hot, interminable climb, and then one last descent that delivered me, exhausted, into the forecourt of the Hotel Terminus St Jacques in Figeac.

Here I had a little luck, for Jacques Morenas, who runs this neat hotel by the station, is a follower of St James. One look at my scallop-shell and he was all assistance. The bike was wheeled away, my panniers carried upstairs, I was helped to the bar, and my pre-booked room changed (I suspect) for a better one. The St Jacques is full of Compostela memorabilia, maps of the roads on the walls, silver scallop-shells hang in the bar, the cross of the Knights of Santiago is painted on the hotel signboard — and the pilgrims pass by on their way to Compostela.

'We had another journalist pass by earlier this year with his teenage son, both on foot. They had left Le Puy on Christmas Day.'

'Christmas Day! In winter? How did they cross the Aubrac in winter? Did they make it to Santiago?'

Jacques shrugged his shoulders. 'They made it to here. I expect they managed it. And we had another journalist here a few days ago, on a bike like you, a lady from Lyon. What is it about St Jacques that attracts you journalists?'

That lady from Lyon again, doing better than I was in this heat apparently. We finished the bottle and, having arranged for an early start next morning, I went wearily to bed.

Figeac is a pretty little town on the Celé, chiefly noted as the birthplace of two diverse characters, firstly Champollion, who deciphered the Rosetta Stone and so solved the riddle of Eygptian hieroglyphics, and that romantic actor of the late war years, Charles Boyer. There are some fine old buildings, including the Hotel de la Monnaie, an old mint, and a small version of Cleopatra's Needle outside the Church of St Sauveur in memory of Champollion. The town would dearly love to have the Rosetta Stone, but that was wrested from the baggage of a French General, and now lies in the British Museum. Even Champollion had to work from a plaster replica.

There is little in Figeac to delay the Compostela pilgrim, but there is a choice. Just a short way to the north-west lies the site of Rocamadour, one of the great pilgrim centres of France and a favourite stop on the Road. Otherwise the pilgrim can continue directly on the journey and head for the next major stop at Cahors, down the valley of the Celé.

Rocamadour is famous for the shrine of St Amadour, and contains, like Le Puy, another of those rare Black Virgins in a grotto set high above the Alzou canyon. Rocamadour clings to the side of this gorge, a fantastic sight. Rebuilt in the last century after great destruction during the Wars of Religion and the Revolution, it still has a power to impress the eye, which is almost physical. I had been to Rocamadour several times, and would have liked to go there again, but diversions are hard for the true pilgrim, even one on a good bike. I reflected on the trials of the last few days and struck out directly for Cahors.

Keeping to my new found resolve, I left the St Jacques before dawn, riding out through empty streets and turning off for the south just as the first mild rays of the sun were shredding the mist above the river. This is a pretty, shady trail, through the Val-Paradis beside the Celé, and since it follows a river the road is mercifully flat and runs gently through some small, attractive villages and towns. I even had breath to whistle.

Espagnac-St-Eulalie was still asleep when I rode through, but it was well worth a stop. It is said to be the prettiest village

The abbey at Marcilhac

in Quercy, which may well be the case. The church has a charming wooden belltower and contains medieval effigies of the local lords.

At Marcilhac, eye still cocked to the rising sun, I had breakfast at a small, fly-infested café, after which, leaving my bike in the care of the old lady proprietor, wandered down to view the old abbey. Most of this is in ruins, but what remains is a pleasing mixture of the Gothic and the Romanesque, and the cloisters contain a rather crude statue of St James, a reminder that Marcilhac too, lies on the Road to Compostela. Indeed, the Abbot once controlled the shrine at Rocamàdour and gained great profit, but the English destroyed the abbey at the end of the fourteenth century and it never revived.

A little past here lies Cabrerets, an attractive town beside the river, with a large *château-fort* facing the Devil's Castle, an English stronghold across the river. The caves of the grotte-du-Pech-Merle, like those of Lascaux a little to the north, contain prehistoric cave paintings. Just south of Cabrerets the Celé runs into the Lot, and I turned west again, following the main road to Vers and arrived by noon in the small village of Laroque. The sun was hitting hard against my back but Cahors was already in sight so, feeling myself wise for once, I rewarded myself with lunch in the little restaurant St Roch, which is tucked away beside the road beneath the pilgrim chapel. By the early afternoon I was riding into Cahors, bowling along before a strong gusting wind.

Cahors is an old fortress town, the pride and capital of Quercy, famous for its wine and that medieval masterpiece, the Pont Valentré. I rode up to the bridge along the riverside esplanade, in the shade of great plane trees being rapidly stripped of their bark by the scouring buffets of wind. Cahors occupies a neck of land surrounded by a great loop of the Lot. Defending the medieval town was therefore fairly easy, for a wall could be built across the narrow neck of land, the river served in the office of a moat, and the only exit south was by this fortified bridge, the Pont Valentré. Today there are other, less attractive bridges, but the Pont still carries traffic and looks marvellous, glaring white in the afternoon sun. It was built about 1308 and the story goes that the mason entrusted with the work and under bond to complete it on time, soon realised that he would never manage it without supernatural assistance. He therefore made a pact with the Devil, in which Satan would see that the bridge was completed on time and, most important, obey all the instructions of the mason, who put up his soul in exchange. The work went well, and the bridge was soon nearing completion, at which point the mason began to fear for his future. Then he had a brainwave; he ordered the Devil to fetch water for the workers — and handed him a sieve. Furious at being cheated out of his prize, the Devil went to the top of the central tower, still called the Tower of the Devil, and hurled down stones upon the workforce far below.

Well, it may be so, why not? The bridge was the bastion of the town's defenses, and still has three of the five original towers. The landward walls are also imposing, and buttressed by the Tour des Pendus, the Hanging Tower, where executions were carried out beside the road. The town once belonged to the Templars and after their extirpation by Philipe IV it passed into the hands of the English after the Treaty of Brétigny in 1360, who held it for nearly a hundred years. For many years power lay in the hands of the Bishop, who held the secular as well as the ecclisiastical lordship and displayed his helmet, sword and steel gauntlets on the cathedral altar to remind the citizens of his total authority.

Today, Cahors, the birthplace of Gambetta,is the capital of Quercy, one of the most delightful corners of France and a trading centre for the famous local wine, the so-called Black Wine of Quercy, and no meal here is complete without a bottle of the 'bon Cahors'. The Romans brought these vines to the steep hillsides of the Lot valley, and it was the rich local vintages which brought the English invaders from nearby Périgord during the Hundred Years' War, when Cahors was regularly besieged.

Until the Revolution of 1917, Cahors was the Communion wine of the Russian Orthodox Church, and when this great

The author by the Pont Valantré, Cohors

market collapsed the local *vignerons* suffered a setback from which they are only now recovering. Quercy is one of those delightful little-known provinces of France, dotted with small villages, where sheep graze on the low *causses*, and dovecotes stand in every farmyard, each with its flock of fluttering pigeons.

This was a pleasant day, an easy meander down the Celé and I arrived at the Hotel Melchior, just by the station, in mid-afternoon, then strolled about the town, head bowed against that scouring wind, to the Cathedral of St Etienne, which has those Périgordianne cupolas and a much-damaged cloister. Cahors is just a little place, with only 20,000 inhabitants, but it seems lively, the main street lined with busy cafés, so I dined early and well, with the inevitable bottle of 'bon Cahors'; packed again and loaded my bicycle, and made ready for another quick half-day's spring to the next major point on my journey, the town of Moissac, on the next river I had to cross, the Tarn. I went to bed that night wondering about the continual absence of other pilgrims.

*   *   *

The Road to Moissac leads out over the Pont Valentré, which is as it should be. Then it turns east beside the river, past the Fontaine de Chartreux, a Roman shrine which still supplies Cahors with fresh water. South of the river lies the limestone country of the *Quercy Blanc*, a region of low hills, which are easy to climb in low gear on a cool morning. A quiet minor road led to the hilltown of Lauzerte, where I arrived for breakfast in rising rain. Rain — how delightful! It seemed to be ages since I had seen rain, and anything seemed better than the ever-relentless sun. I cranked up to Lauzerte, puffing out 'To be a Pilgrim' to prove I was fit, and feeling valiant, marched soggily into a café and demanded breakfast. If there are finer pleasures than a big cup of *café au lait* on a wet morning, I couldn't think of one at the time. Lauzerte is a *bastide*, one of those thirteenth-century fortified towns, built to defend the march of Aquitaine. From Lauzerte it seemed no time at all to Moissac on the Tarn, racing along the road, the rain rattling on my windproofs, finally rolling to a halt outside the Hotel Chapon-Fin just before noon, while a thunderstorm broke above the roofs of the town and the rain came sheeting down, with seventy fresh kilometres under my wheels that morning and not a sign of strain. Yvan Conoir from La Dépêche du Midi turned up at the Chapon-Fin for dinner and Jean Conovar, the manager, heard of my journey so far, with a gratifying amount of admiration. 'It's not the Tour de France,' he said, 'but still....' Things were looking up.

* * *

Moissac is famous for its abbey, another Cluniac foundation. Much of the original abbey has been destroyed and what remains narrowly escaped total extinction in the last century

The doorway at the abbey, Moissac

The cloisters, Moissac Abbey

Detail of the abbey doorway, Moissac

A capital in the cloisters at Moissac

when the engineers surveying the Bordeaux-Séte railway found it lying directly in their path; luckily they were diverted by the Beaux-Arts and the tracks now run just behind the cloisters. The abbey church of St Pierre lies in the centre of the town, reached through an untidy clutter of streets, but the impact of the building is immediate, a vast, bulking fortified tower, the nave part Romanesque stone, part Gothic brick. The storm had cleared people from the square, the light had that curious grey glow that comes from thunder, and the doors stood open, dark beneath the vast carved tympanum. I stood out in the open street and took my first good hard look at a Compostela pilgrim church. I had seen several others by now, but at times when I had been tired or out of sorts, and this one, seen when fairly fresh, made an immediate impression. The original abbey building was clearly Romanesque, but the great door is a mixture of Cluniac and Mozarabic art, marked with the influences of France and Spain, which is as it should be on the Road to Compostela.

The portals are curved and jagged, a feature I grew used to south of the Pyrénées, for such curves are the mark of Mozarabic work, which was created by Christian masons or architects influenced by the horseshoe-shaped loops popular in Moorish or Visigothic buildings. The doorway at Moissac is said to be influenced by craftsmen who had worked on, or seen, those at Santo Domingo de Los Silos, but wherever the idea came from the result is striking. The doors are flanked by these carved panels, and divided by pillars formed from pairs of rampart, clawing, interwoven lions, the whole topped by that striking Cluniac tympanum which draws its inspiration here from the Book of Revelation.

'...and a door was opened in Heaven before the splendour of the Lord and behold, a throne was set and One sat upon the throne. And there was a rainbow about the throne like unto an emerald; and round the throne were four and twenty seats and upon the seats I saw four and twenty elders sitting, clothed in white rainment, with crowns of gold upon their heads, playing on viols.'

And so it is at Moissac. Christ sits in majesty, surrounded by the evangelists and the elders of the Apocalypse, supported by St Peter and Isaiah. It is an amazing and lyrical sight, and it served to instruct as well as beautify. Medieval churches were carved and painted and supplied with statues, not just to glorify God's House but so that these items could be used to educate the congregation in a time when few could read. They served, it is said, as the 'Bibles of the poor', who could see the faces and fates of the saints in their church and draw on the morals pointed out by the clergy.

Lord Clark, the art historian, once wrote that the sculptor of Moissac must have been '...an eccentric of the first order, a sort of Romanesque El Greco.' He was almost certainly a 'free-mason', one of those craftsmen who, because of his skill, was protected by the Church or the great lords and could travel from place to place, free from the normal restrictions imposed by the secular lords or the trade guilds. Certainly this one shares much with the other great tympana of the Road, at Autun perhaps, or Vézelay, and it provides a fitting, if overwhelming, start to a tour of this fine building.

The Moorish elements here are also fascinating, and serve as a reminder that the flow of ideas down the Road to Compostela was not a one-way trade. It is true that the

Gothic made its way into Spain down the Chemin de St Jacques, but the art of the Road, notably the Romanesque, owes much of its distribution to the pilgrims who spread it even as far as England. The Norman church at Kilpeck, near Hereford, is decorated in a style reminiscent of the pilgrim churches of Saintogne, and those who look about the parish churches of England will often find ideas or decoration which might well have been gleaned by travellers on the Road. Romanesque grows on you; at first it seems too solid and heavy to charm the eye, lacking the soaring verticality of the Gothic, but it has great charm.

Much of the present Church of St Pierre is Gothic and dates from about 1450, but the cloisters are pure Romanesque. This term has nothing to do with the Romans, but draws its name from the supposedly 'romantic' flowing nature of the decoration. The cloisters at Moissac are in excellent repair and date from the original Cluniac foundation in the eleventh century. Each pillar is carved and decorated in the purest Romanesque while the central lawn is overshadowed by a vast cedar of Lebanon.

Th cloister was empty on this dark afternoon; rain dripped heavily from the eaves, black clouds towered over the roof of the church and it was all rather eerie. Perhaps it was the darkness, perhaps the sudden stillness of the air, but I felt a sense of — what? Something hard to define. I am not the sensitive type but I wrote in my notebook that I suddenly felt 'odd'. I came to know this feeling well, though it stayed with me longer and more strongly later. It was that first touch of time's continuum, a glimpse of the spirit of the Road. I shrugged it off and hurried out into the drying streets, away from the shadows that might be imagined flitting about the ancient cloisters in the pilgrim church of Moissac.

Chapter 4
The Road to the Pyrénées

'Au coeur avions si grand desir
De voir Saint-Jacques
Avons laisse tous nos plaisirs
Pour faire ce voyage.'

Grande Chanson des
Pélerins de St-Jacques

A French cyclist I met in Cahors warned me about the hills of the Gers. *'C'est pénible,'* he said. I had half-decided, in a moment of weakness, to veer away from my present route and cut south to the Pyrénées through Toulouse.

This is still a valid route for many pilgrims chose to pass by Toulouse to visit the great Church of St Sernin, the largest Romanesque church in the Midi, full of powerful relics. The outside is currently in need of restoration but the inside is splendid; there was a church here in the fourth century, and the present building, commenced around 1080, took over three hundred years to complete. The Miégeville door has a fine tympanum; the coffins of those Counts of Toulouse denied burial in holy ground for supporting the Albigensians rest in the porch, and the crypt once held the relics of many venerable saints, presented to the church by Charlemagne: St Philip, St James the Less, St Gilbert, St Edmund (these last two being English), and, it was once believed, those of our own St James of Compostela, news which alarmed Dr Boorde when he arrived here in the sixteenth century.

The nave contains a splendid reliquary to my favourite saint, St Jude, the patron saint of lost causes. St Jude became the saint people turned to when all else failed because when all the saints were being adopted by various groups of people — St Cicelia by musicians, St Nicolas by sailors and pawnbrokers — nobody wanted to be represented by St Jude. His name was too easily confused with that of Judas, and nobody

Early morning mist at Flamarens

thought *his* intercession would do any good. St Jude found himself unemployed and was happy to take on any task he could get.

I like the red city of Toulouse, but looking at the map, I did not see how the hills ahead could be as punishing as the journey so far, crossing the valleys of the great rivers which already lay behind. A word is always useful to the wise, so I crept out of the Chapon Fin well before daylight and struck out for the south through a deep mist, determined to knock off as much distance as possible early in the day.

Much of this morning mist came from the rivers, first from the Tarn, then briefly from the Canal-lateral-de-la-Garonne, and finally from the Garonne itself. I was soon damp and then wet through with dew, coated with little drops which clung to the hair on my arms and legs. At Pommavic I crossed the Garonne and wandered south on some very minor roads to St Antoine, making very good time over flat country and looking forward to another fast and easy day. Gradually, though, the land changed.

The Gers, which lies to the west of the city of Toulouse, stretching as far as the flat country of the Landes, is a tumbled, jumbled region, a maze of small hills and little rivers. This is Gascony, the home of D'Artagnan, where the main occupation is growing grapes for the production of Armagnac. During the course of that day those steep little vine-draped hills gradually broke my back. They are in truth relentless, even *pénible*, but there are compensations.

Flamarens is one compensation, half-abandoned, half-empty village, with a medieval *château-fort* in the Gascon style rearing its towers out of the silky morning fog. Miradoux is pretty and a kind lady in a café there served me coffee and dried out my dew-soaked anorak over her kitchen stove; and Lectoure is almost perfect. I reached there about ten o'clock in the morning as the mist finally shredded away and the sun came out to paint the countryside with colour.

Lectoure is a hill town, standing high above the river Gers, which gives its name to this *département*. It is one of those towns which time has knocked about a bit, and something most curious has happened to the cathedral which appears to have been bitten in half, the effect of a cannonade during the

The cathedral at Lectoure

65

Wars of Religion. There are fine views over the countryside from the promenade as far as the Pyrénées on a clear day. Lectoure is the birthplace of Marshal Lannes, one of Napolean's comrades in arms, who joined the Revolutionary Army in 1792 and became a general three years later; promotion was clearly rapid in those reeling days. He was killed at Essling in 1809, but his home in the *château* here which was, in its time, the home of the Counts of Armagnac, contains an interesting Napoleonic museum. Lectoure is a pleasing, busy little town and I whiled away most of the morning there before rushing down the hill to the river Gers and beginning the long cross-country slog to Condom. My diary describes the road to Condom as 'a brute'; it is one of those routes which motorists might find attractive but cyclists hate. Given low gears, and once the legs get strong, long ascents hold few terrors for the cycle-tourist. Just keep turning the pedals and sooner or later the top of the hill will come in sight and then, with luck, you have the reward of a long refreshing descent. The hills of the Gers are not like that; they are short, steep, coated with gravel-chippings, and follow each other as relentlessly as waves on the surface of the sea.

Condom lies on a hill set in a broad valley, and I arrived on market day, pushing my bike through the square by the cathedral which was full of stalls and striped awnings. The outer walls of St Pierre seemed to be crumbling but the inside is in wonderful condition, with a splendid chancel and beautiful heraldic bosses set high in the vault of the nave. I bought a melon and ate it sitting in the sunshine on the bridge by the Boise, and tried out the local speciality, a *pousse-rapière*, a 'sword-thrust', a mix of Armagnac and white wine, before leaving Condom for my next destination, Larressingle.

Larressingle is a small fortified village, 5km west of Condom. Larressingle is a beauty and small is not really the word for it; minute is better. The village stands on a hill, surrounded by high walls, and it took me just three minutes to walk around the edge of the now dry moat. I love old walled places and France is full of them, but I know of none as lovely as Larressingle. It was fortified during the Middle Ages by the local bishop, and the villagers took shelter there when the English came storming past, raiding the march of Gascony. It was beseiged several times, but seems to have suffered very little and I spent a very happy hour poking about the little streets, cooling off in the Romanesque church, or admiring the defences of the castle. A cannon post looks out directly on the main gate, and at the upper level church and castle were once clearly linked. Today the little village dreams in the sun, the warm golden walls draped with madly drooping hollyhocks. I was sorry to leave.

* * *

The pilgrim road and the GR65 overlap each other after Condom and the hills of the Gers relent a little, influenced by the flatter country of the Landes now butting in from the

The author at Larresingle

west. The rest of the day was hot but pleasant, a steady ride all the way to my night stop at Eauze, after having covered over 110km across some fairly tough and tumbled country. Eauze is a rather grubby town, the capital of the Armagnac, but it grows on you, a little. I hid from the evening heat in the bar which now occupies the Maison Jeanne d'Albret. Here, according to a plaque on the wall, Henry of Navarre and his Queen, Margarite, once spent seventeen days recovering from a fever. I felt quite sorry for them in the time I could spare from feeling sorry for myself. Solitary travellers should get used to feeling lonely, and some even prefer it, but sometimes it creeps up on you. Besides, it seemed ridiculous. I was travelling through one of the pleasantest and most populated countries in Europe, yet for all the human contact I was having, I might have been crossing the Sahara. I hadn't spoken anything but French for a week, or discussed anything more stimulating than the weather; and the weather was heating up again, I thought sourly, stamping back to the Hotel Henri IV, a rather dilapidated hostelry which appeared to be run entirely by children. They were pleasant enough, even quite efficient in their own way, but they lay about the place in little heaps and had a tendency to stare.

Sunk in my bath, I contemplated my woes, which multiplied. A very large wasp appeared, orbited the taps and disappeared. Another did likewise, then a third. I peered worriedly over the rim and saw two more crawling busily up the tiled wall from beneath the sink. Splashing about stark naked next to a hornets' nest was an unnecessary extra; I swept downstairs to make a scene and did terrible things over dinner to a bottle of the local *Buzet*.

Getting up at five-thirty always seems a good idea, except at five-thirty. I crept into the bathroom, anxious not to wake the wasps, and contemplated my cracked and sunburnt face in the mirror. That sun of yesterday must have been stronger than I had thought. I studied my blistered lips, now swelling nicely, and decided to defer starting trumpet lessons for a few days more. When I returned to my bedroom to dress, a large cockroach was labouring up the wall past my pillow. I gave up and left hurriedly for the Pyrénées.

The castle at Morlanne

One way to get rid of a depression is to work it to death. I stormed across country to Nogaro, whirling over the hills and raced on to Aire-sur-l'Adour in time for breakfast, bounded back into the saddle full of vim and *café au lait*, and shot south to Geaune, Pimbo, (forcing myself into great good humour), and into Arzacq-Arraziguet just in time for lunch. Rob was himself again, and cheered not a little by the sight, still dim but definitely getting closer, of the snow-tipped Pyrénées, now looming up to the south, across the misty valley of the *gave de Pau*.

Arzacq is a pin-bright little town, the whitewashed houses sensibly equipped with shady verandahs, and I particularly liked the poker-work motto in one of the bars: 'Men are like melons; you have to try ten before you find one worth having'; all in all, a good place to wait out the heat of the day before riding on towards Arthez-de-Bearn, past Morlanne

69

The church at Morlanne

with its splendid fourteenth-century castle. I met a man in the street here who inspected my cockle-shell closely, enquired if I was going to St Jacques, and then insisted on talking to me in Spanish which, added to his local patois brought comprehension to a halt. He bade me '*bon route*' and I forged on to Arthez, climbing up the final ridge to look down on the valley of the *gave de Pau* and across to the Pyrénées. There lay Spain, and the mid-point of my journey. I tipped over the crest, rushed down to the valley and into the village of Maslacq.

* * *

That evening in Maslacq I pondered the absence of pilgrims. so far, apart from the odd walker, I had met no one, and heard only of this cycling lady from Lyon who remained little more than a rumour, flitting across the landscape somewhere ahead, leaving brief notes in visitors' books; and yet this was a Holy Year, one of those when the Feast of St James fell on a Sunday, and some two million pilgrims were expected in

Santiago. Counting the lady and myself, where were the other one million, nine hundred and ninety-nine thousand, nine hundred and ninety eight? I had been eight days on the Road, and the Road was empty.

In some ways this was not surprising, for there, are, and always were, many roads to Compostela. If all the pilgrims had gone down one route, they would have swept it bare of provisions as efficiently as a swarm of locusts. The pilgrimage is best imagined not as a convoy but a general drift, a popular annual migration, as the pilgrims made their way west along old Roman roads, on little tracks, along the traditional *drailles* or drove roads, meeting only at such major shrines as Conques or Moissac or in the face of danger, as on the Aubrac, then gradually banding together to cross the Pyrénées.

Two main passes carried the pilgrim traffic over the Pyrénées, the Somport south of Oleron-Ste-Marie, which leads from Béarn over the mountains and down to Jaca and Huesca, and the pass of Roncesvalles which led from St-Jean-Pied-de-Port to Pamplona. Here at Maslacq I still had a choice but the decision followed tradition, for the Somport is the route for those pilgrims who come from St Gilles, and mine lay west, towards St Palais in the Basque country, where the roads from Le Puy, Vézelay and Paris come together. Here, with luck, more pilgrims should appear.

The road to St Palais was delightful, but the weather was otherwise. It began pleasantly enough with a short run in the sunshine into Orthez, and stayed bright long enough for me to persuade someone to take my photograph as I rode to and fro across the fine fortified bridge that spans the *gave*. Then it began to rain. Orthez was the capital of Béarn, that great medieval lordship which produced Gaston Phoebus and Henry of Navarre. The mighty Counts of Foix built the bridge and most of the still existing fortifications. Orthez is a rather splendid town, even when rain is rushing down the gutters and flooding into the turbulent waters of the *gave de Pau*, but I had to press on, butting through the storm to Sauveterre over the pilgrim road to the chapel at l'Hopital d'Orion. You enter this little church through a tangle of bell

The fortified bridge at Orthez

ropes, into the place where Gaston Phoebus died of apoplexy in 1390, and stand on a spot where pilgrims have knelt for nearly a thousand years.

Sauveterre-de-Béarn which, from the name, was built as a

Romanesque church at Sauveterre-de-Béarn

A fortified bridge at Sauveterre-de-Béarn

bastide, is a fine little town on the *gave d' Oleron*, perched high on a cliff above the river. There are the remains of a fine medieval castle, a very well preserved church, and yet another of those fortified bridges, although the one here has been half destroyed. In 1170 this was the scene of a curious trial, when the King of Navarre got it into his head that his sister Sancia, widow of the Count of Foix, was a witch. He had her tied hand and foot, then thrown from the bridge into the river. Had she floated she would have been brought ashore and burnt, but she sank like a stone. Dragged out half-drowned, she was met by her delighted brother and restored to her estates!

Sauveterre lies on the pilgrim road to Roncesvalles, which runs from here across the green hills and into the country of the Basques at St Palais, and as the pilgrim rides the last few miles from Béarn into Basse-Navarre it is quickly apparent that the Basques are different. Their language, 'Euskara', which now appears on the road signs, is completely incomprehensible; they say that the Devil tried to learn it for seven years then gave up in disgust. Every village has its 'fronton' or pelota court, every church its graveyard with those distinctive round Basque tombstones carved with jaw-cracking Basque names. the Basques, French or Spanish, are most clearly one people, and their country, the Kingdom of Navarre, once spanned the Pyrénées with Pamplona as the capital. The four provinces south of the Pyrénées were annexed by Ferdinand of Castile in 1512 and the three northern ones, Labourd, Basse-Navarre and Soule, were attached to France when Henry of Navarre became Henry IV, although all seven still remain distinctly Basque. This trans-Pyrénéan kingdom was very useful to the Compostela pilgrims, since it provided them with a bridge across the mountains from the fairly familiar France into the mysterious heart of Spain.

St Palais lies on the Bidouze and I turned off by the bridge and rode into the campsite by the river. After carrying a tent across France it seemed time to start using it, and anyway, my funds would not support too many more nights in hotels. I found an enormous pitch under the dripping trees, put up the tent, stowed my kit inside and set off to explore the town,

A game of 'fronton' in the Basque country

beginning with a very good lunch at the Hotel Trinquet, where, happy sight, several bikes were parked against the wall, each bearing on the handlebars the *coquille de St Jacques*. More pilgrims at last!

St Palais is a Franco-Basque town, full on this Saturday afternoon with carloads of Basques setting off for Pamplona and the San Firman festival. Most seemed to be already in the state which journalists tactfully describe as 'tired and emotional', so after dodging their cars and periodic cloud-bursts, I took shelter in a bar at the foot of the road to Mont St Sauveur, and waited out the afternoon watching the Wimbledon finals on the television in the corner, while chatting to Madame Castillon, the proprietress, another friend of St Jacques.

'Tout le monde va a Compostelle cette année,' she told me cheerfully, stacking glasses on the shelves behind the bar.

'Really? I've been on the Road for over a week and not seen a soul.'

'Oh yes, lots. We've seen many walkers, but they passed long ago now. We even had a party on horseback. Now we have cyclists. There was a lady here this morning....'

'Not from Lyon?'

'*Oui... je pense....* Yes, from Lyon.'

Well, at least it looked more hopeful. I had gained four days on the lady from Lyon; the Roads to Compostela were coming together and if I made an early start I might overhaul other pilgrims and find a little company. All in all it was a cheerful evening, until I tottered back to the campsite and found that my tent had collapsed. Fighting wet nylon in a high wind and rain is never easy. My efforts to re-erect the tent were watched with great interest by the other campers, but eventually a group of Germans, unable to stand the sight any longer, came over, pushed me aside and had the tent up in a trice. Looking helpless can sometimes have advantages. I crawled inside, beat my sleeping bag into submission, and fell asleep.

Chapter 5
The Road to Pamplona

'There's no discouragement,
Shall make him once relent
His first avowed intent
To be a pilgrim.'

John Bunyan

It rained hard all night. Snug in my tent, well stunned by the
local wine, I slept through the gale except when a particularly
violent gust of wind shook my shelter and sent a fine spray of
rain through the thin walls on to my face. That roused me for
a second or so but the rain died out before dawn and I dozed
on for another couple of hours before stirring myself and
peeping out at the day.

The day was dreay. Large grey clouds were roaming
overhead, large drops plopped down from the trees and the
earth steamed. It promised to be one of those hot, muggy,
enervating days which self-propelled travellers can well do
without. There is a rule for such occasions, which dictates
that the traveller leaps from his sleeping bag, plunges into
cold shower or mountain stream, and thus refreshed, sets out
to meet the day head on. I have never managed to obey this
rule.

I crawled out, grumpy, cursing the wet grass, cursing the
wet, flapping folds of the tent, cursing my damp clothes and
rapidly rusting cookset, cursing the cheery Germans drinking
coffee and waving from the big tent opposite. Why didn't
they help now? They were quick enough to interfere last
night! Cramming wet bundles into my panniers, I rode off
into town and sought comfort from Madame Castillon. She,
too, was cheerful, morning cheerfulness being one of the
professional hotelier's more irritating habits, but she poured
me large cups of coffee and offered croissants without more
than a nod. Eventually I began to revive, and seeing this, she
began to urge me onwards.

The road to Gibraltar

'If you hurry,' she offered, 'you will catch the lady from Lyon. She was only a few hours ahead of you yesterday and must have stopped nearby.'

'I've lost interest in the lady from Lyon. Besides, there are lots of things to see between here and St Jean. May I leave my panniers here while I ride up to Gibraltar?'

Gibraltar is a curious name for a hilltop in the Basque country, but the locals claim that it is a corruption of the French name Mont St Sauveur, which, if correct, gives some idea of the distortions created by the Basque tongue. The Gibraltar of the Straits can be easily linked to the Arabic name Jebel-el-Tariq, but this one seems less likely.

Pondering this, I took the road from St Palais to the crossroads at Gibraltar. This road goes straight up the side of Mont-St-Sauveur, a stiff climb to start the day but worth it for the Compostela pilgrim. This hilltop is the point where three

The stele at Gibraltar

of the old Roads meet, those coming from Paris, Vézelay and Le Puy — or so some will have it. Others disagree.

The site certainly looks right, with footpaths coming over the hills from the north and east, linking into a broad track which leads up to the summit, and the modern obelisk which marks the spot has the signs and scallop-shells of St James, but as I was photographing all this, a man appeared from the farmhouse opposite and began to shout at me.

'*C'est faux,*' he cried. '*C'est faux!*'

'What is?' I asked.

Apparently the site was. According to this local resident, who never offered his name, the real Road ran south, along the valley and the trails joined at Ostabat — that was obvious and sensible, wasn't it? Who would climb hills and stay on the tops when it was easier going down below and close to water for the horses and pack-mules? Valleys can, of course, be choked with undergrowth, boggy and prone to flooding. There is scope for different views, but I will stick with the authorities who maintain that these Gibraltar crossroads above St Palais are the first junction of the Roads. Climbing back into the saddle, I freewheeled speedily back to Madame Castillon's bar, collected my luggage, said goodbye, and set off south for St-Jean-Pied-de-Port and Spain.

*   *   *

The day developed as predicted, drizzly, hot and muggy. Cars full of white-clad Basques poured past in clouds of spray, and I was quite glad when one of those now rapidly-appearing 'Camino de Santiago' signs drew me to the left a few kilometres down the road, taking me away from the road through the Bois de Ostabat, along a rapidly deteriorating woodland path to the hamlet of Harambels. The pilgrim chapel at Harambels has been there for a thousand years, a small tiled-roof barn of a place, with a triple belltower over all. The key is kept in the house opposite, and the interior of the Chapel of St Nicolas is well worth seeing, with painted walls, various statues, including one of a Compostela pilgrim, and a well-worn retable painted in fading hues of red and gold. St Nicolas is one of the oldest pilgrim churches in Western Europe. It was built at least a thousand years ago and Ameri Picaud mentions it and the inhabitants of the village in his *Liber Sancti Jacobi* in the *Codex Calixtinus* of 1149. There were four families living here in the twelfth century, Borda, Etcheto, Etcheverry and Salla, and these names are still those recorded in the churchyard just across the way, a connection with the distant past.

Through the woods lies the village of Ostabat itself, another stop on the Pilgrim Way, reached by a path across a ford. I returned to the main road and rode round to the village, and on this Sunday morning Ostabat seemed a lively place after little Harambels, with all the people coming out of church. Ostabat also claims to be a main junction of the Road and once had twenty hostels to shelter Compostela pilgrims, but now has only one bar, although the locals are very friendly. The priest flagged me down, heard my tale and, disappearing into his church, soon returned with a rubber stamp to mark my notebook, as proof of passage.

'There were four other pilgrims here this morning,'he said. 'All *en vélo*, like you.' None, apparently, was the lady from Lyon, and when I stopped for more coffee at Larceveau, a little further on, she had not been there either. Curious!

* * *

The twenty miles between St Palais and St Jean took most of the morning, but the ride was interesting, along the banks of the rushing Bidouze over an undulating road. Bamboo flourishes here in deep thickets and, stopping at the first bridge, I saw a kingfisher flash past underneath the arch and perch a little way downstream, a brilliant spot of colour against the stones. Crashing down through the undergrowth just after the second bridge, I found the stepping-stones where the GR65 footpath, *Le Chemin de St Jacques*, crosses the river before climbing up the hill towards Gibraltar. These stepping stones across the Bidouze are vast circular affairs, hewn from the rock and, like so many useful things along the Road, have probably been there for a thousand years or more.

Thus diverted, I rolled heavily on, flagging in the sticky heat until the Road kinked right at St-Jean-le-Vieux and brought me directly into the frontier town of St-Jean-Pied-de-Port.

The little town of 'St-John-at-the-Foot-of-the-Pass' is a pretty place and very historic. I like it all; the Vauban fortress, the red walls and rooftops, the great church of Notre-Dame-du-Pont by the river Nive, the steep, narrow street of the rue de la Citadele leading down from the Porte St Jacques. Most of all, I like the Hotel des Pyrénées, one of the nicest places to stay in Southern France, staffed and managed by the friendliest of Basques — and I like the Basques. Picaud didn't. He writes about them in his *Guide du Pelerin*, and says nothing in their favour. 'A barbarous people, full of trickery, black of colour, drunken, expert in all violence....' He goes on and on about them and concludes that they will kill you for a *sou*.

Aubrac

Espalion

Estaing on the River Lot

The pilgrim track at Noailhac

Houses by the River Nive, St-Jean-Pied-de-Port

Times have changed, however, for although the Hotel des Pyrénées is rather a refined place, the staff are helpful, even to unkempt cyclists. Within ten minutes the cycle was secure in a garage, my damp clothes were drying on a line, my wet tent was draped over a wall, and I was draped over a bottle of *Irouleguy*, the Basque country's most drinkable wine, awaiting the hotel's great speciality, *jambon piperade*, eggs and ham in a spicy cheese sauce, which was quite delicious. The wine had me worried though, for the label was marked with an alarming Basque instruction, **HOXZ HOTZA EDAM!** Now what can *that* mean, I wondered? 'Serve slightly chilled' was the answer. Of course.

Thus fortified, if a trifle unsteady, I set out to see the sights and began by entering the old town through the Porte St Jacques, and searching for Madame Debril, one of the great characters of the Road, well known to passing pilgrims. I finally bumped into her standing in the rain outside a shop. Madame Debril is the chronicler of the true pilgrims who pass through St Jean. She will supply them with a small passport, declaring their status as a *Peregrino del Camino de Santiago*, and makes the first entry, recording their arrival at St Jean.

81

Other stamps, obtained along the Way, at Val-Carlos, Pamplona, Estella, Burgos, Fromista, and so on, prove that the true pilgrim has followed the Way of St James, and the Cathedral Secretariat in Santiago will thereon grant that precious *compostelle*.

That apart, Madame Debril records the passing of the pilgrims every year, and is a great historian. She took me into her study, where numerous cats leapt and slid about among piles of books and papers, and we filled in the details of my journey for her files. Over 700 true pilgrims had already passed through that year, but only one from England, a girl on foot, Jocelyn Rix from Birmingham who had passed through weeks before; no note here of the lady from Lyon.

'I don't see them all,' said Madame Debril, throwing another cat out of the ground-floor window. 'Some just ride straight through, or go to St Jean and the Col de Cize on foot.

Notre -Dame-du-Pont, St-Jean-Pied-de-Port, from the Rue St Jacques

You must tell them to stop here and get their passport.' I said I would and took my leave, stepping delicately over the cats and out into the present capital of Basse-Navarre, homeland of Basques.

St Jean seemed to be full of Basques, tricked out in the traditional white clothes, red berets and sashes, standing around in groups in the rain, waiting to head south to the San Firmin fiesta at Pamplona. No one really knows where the Basques came from. They were already here in this land which straddles the Pyrénées when the Romans came, and their language, Euskara, which is the normal clue to tribal identity, is no help whatsoever. Voltaire said 'The Basques are a little people who dance at the foot of the Pyrénées,' while Victor Hugo remarked, more kindly, that 'The Basques know all of the sea and the mountains,' and he may have been right. Columbus's pilot on the *Santa Maria* was a Basque, but then he did not know where he was going. On the other hand, it was a Basque who brought Magellan's ship home after the first circumnavigator was killed in the Philippines. Basque shipwrights at Bayonne built ships for the Armada, and there are Basque communities all over the world, from Nevada to Patagonia, all speaking Euskara and dancing the fandango.

The Porte St Jacques is a medieval gateway marking the pilgrim road through St Jean and overlooked by a much later Vauban fortress. Coming through the gate the traveller at once enters the Vieille Ville and a narrow street which leads steeply down to the Nive. On the right side there is a fine wooden doorway studded with small brass cockle-shells, while further down lies the bishop's prison, a dark, dank hole, with chains and fetters still dangling from the walls. Here those captured brigands who had preyed upon pilgrims were locked up by the bishop's guards to await trial and sentence. In the fourteenth century many of these robbers were English men-at-arms, unemployed during the truces of the Hundred Years' War. The Baillie of Estella spent a week in 1318 hunting one notorious rogue, John of London.

There were more pilgrim cycle-tourists here, one old gentleman and several boys, watching the crowds from their table in a café by the river, their handlebar-bags bearing the

coquille de St Jacques. I returned to the Hotel des Pyrénées to pack my panniers carefully and have an early night. Twenty miles a day is no way to climb the high green walls of the Pyrénées.

* * *

At St Jean the pilgrim crossing into Spain by the western pass of the Pyrénées has a choice. One route lies directly south of the town through the hamlet of St-Michel-le-Vieus and directly up, through the woods to the Port de Cize at 1,480m, and then west to the col at Ibãneta. This is the route that walkers follow to this day. The other route, equally valid, lies west of this path, through Arneguy and Val Carlos, the valley of Charles, or Charlemagne. This is the route I took, along the main road, the road to Roncesvalles. One would need to have no sense of history at all and a soul devoid of romance to ignore the pass of Roncesvalles. Like many of the pilgrim roads, it owes its origin to the Romans, and has been used by armies for many thousands of years. The Black Prince marched his army through here in 1367, heading for his last great fight at Najera, and returned a sadder but wiser man, bearing the great red ruby that still glows in the Imperial State Crown, and the chronic sickness which eventually killed him. Wellington led his victorious Peninsula army through Roncesvalles from Spain to his penultimate victory before the walls of Toulouse in 1814, and Compostela pilgrims have chosen to pass this way since the pilgrimage began. All other events apart, this is the place where Roland fell and the paladins of Charlemagne with him, an event which provided the West with the basis for one of the first *chansons de geste* — the 'Song of Roland'.

The event itself is reasonably well recorded. About the year 777, Charlemagne led an army into Spain to assist some Moslem princes against their enemies. His army had besieged several cities of Spain with limited success, when an attack by the Saxons on his northern frontier obliged the emperor to return home. As his army was re-crossing the Pyrénées, through Roncesvalles, the Basques set upon the rearguard, which was commanded by the paladin Roland, Lord of the Breton Marches, and slaughtered them to a man. These facts were recorded in AD830 only 60 years after the battle, by the chronicler Eginhardt. Another chronicler even gives the precise date, 15 August 778, all very exactly, but from these certain facts many legends flowed. In the course of a few hundred years, the Basques became Saracens. Roland grew to 7ft in height, Charlemagne became 200 years old, and the battle, though caused by treachery and enhanced by stupidity, was held up as an example to Western Chivalry, their classic defeat. Eventually surrounded by heaps of dead, Roland falls, blowing a last trump on his horn and slashing a great gap in the Pyrénées, the *Breche de Roland,* with one final blow of his magic sword, Durandel. It is all breathtaking stuff, and poets, then and since, have loved it.

Far off . . . a longue *haleine,*
The horn of Roland in the pass of Spain,
The first, the second blast, the failing third,
And with the third turned back and
Climbed once more,
The steep road southward, and heard faint the sound
Of sword, of horses, the disastrous war,
And crossed the dark defile at last and found,
At Roncevaux upon the darkening plain,
The dead against the dead on the
Silent ground,
The silent slain —

*   *   *

Compostela pilgrims setting out from St Jean to cross the Pyrénées, would take with them on this perilous stage of their journey a cross of palm branches, which they would plant on the crest of the mountains above Roncesvalles. In some years, especially in Holy Years, the grassy ground by the Ibeñeta would be furred with such crosses, planted as the pilgrims passed by. I rode out alone from St Jean into little Arneguy on the French side of the frontier, still wondering at the absence of fellow pilgrims along the Road. Stopping at the post office to send some cards, my travel plans, when revealed to the postmaster, got short shrift.

'Crossing Spain on a cycle? In this heat? You must be mad.'

'*Pourquoi?*' I asked. 'I've had a great time so far. What's wrong with Spain, anyway?'

'There are too many Spaniard there.'

'I don't mind that, I like Spaniards.'

'Then you don't know them,' he said darkly, jerking his thumb to the south. 'When they are neighbours . . . you know them.'

*   *   *

Arriving at the frontier a few hundred metres down the road, I began to wonder if he might be right. The Guardia were

Spanish-French border at Val Carlos

standing about on the verandah of the customs' shed in their usual pose of watchful indolence, and I had just ridden past with a wave, when one called after me, 'Are you Belgian?'

'No! *Ingles.*'

That did it! They spilled off the verandah into the road, and hustled me back to the office for a mass interrogation, four of them to one of me.

'Passport? Money? Camera? What's in there? Where are you going? Ah! You're a journalist!' Clearly being a journalist was a bad move.

When a large group of scowling Guardia had gathered round and showed every sign of wanting to unroll and examine all my carefully organised luggage, I tried to divert them by enquiring after the lady from Lyon, and it worked. Hats were removed, heads scratched, a sleeping official prised from his slumbers in the next room, but of the lady from Lyon they had seen no sign. The Spanish have a liking for bureaucracy but unlike the British, thank goodness, they cannot keep it up for long. Cheerfulness began to break through. My passport was returned, my panniers replaced and I was waved on with a chorus of '*Buen viajes*'. This was my only brush with officialdom on the Road to Compostela and be it noted, none of the Guardia was Basque.

*　*　*

From Val Carlos the Road leads up — and up. The northern slopes of the Pyrénées are far steeper than those on the Spanish side, which in some ways is a good thing. My 21km slog from Val Carlos to the Ibeñata would be rewarded on the morrow by a great long swoop, mile after mile without touching the pedals, down to the plains of Nevarre, but that lay ahead. A large plaque beside the Road told me that this indeed was the *Camino de Santiago,* with 805km still to go before the City of St James, and right now I was slogging up the mountainside from Val Carlos, and not enjoying it one bit. I soon gave up attempting to ride and began to plod uphill, pushing my bicycle, gaining height with painful effort and sweating like a pig; and then the horse-flies arrived.

At first I thought it was sweat splashing on to my knee until, looking down, I realised it was blood, a steady drip flowing from my elbow where two large black horse-flies had their heads embedded in veins. Loathsome! Horse-flies, the dreaded Roncesvalles variety, are fearful creatures; shorts and sweater are no armour against them, for they bite straight through. That evening, up at Roncesvalles, when I counted the total number of bites, I found forty-three on the parts I could see, and others elsewhere. They were a torment for most of that day and yet, in some curious perverse way, the pass of Roncesvalles, with the heat, the hills and the incessant goading of the flies, was a high point on the journey, a memorable part of the trip, the day when the true travelling began and I finally cheered up. When the going gets tough, I told myself, the tough get going. Up till then, in spite of the heat and my lack of fitness, it had been just a little too easy to engage the mind, but somewhere on that hill, sometime on that day, I began to get into my stride.

Enough of the pain and suffering; what of the view? Even when seen through sweat-soaked eyelashes, it was, I must confess, not bad. A little extract from the *Song of Roland* may sum it up.

High are the hills, the valleys dark and deep,
Grisly the rocks and wondrous grim the steeps,
Brightly was the day and clearly the sun shone.

Too clearly. The heat was shattering. Fortunately there were plenty of streams cascading down the rocks, into which I paddled, plunged or splashed according to depth, and from time to time there were other small distractions. Carloads of white and red clothed Basques still roared past, cheering me on from the windows; a herd of izard, the Pyrénéan chamois, appeared on a spike of rock high above, then danced across the crags and out of sight. Higher up, where the woods thinned out and the heat became even more appalling, a herd of goats cascaded through the trees, their jangling bells making a frightful din; a large pig appeared on the bank above, slid down the grassy slope on its bottom and proceeded to rootle about for acorns in the ditch at the side of the road. Life wasn't dull. Then I met Jacques Viallard.

I didn't see him at first and, to be honest, I wasn't seeing very much at all by then, except a small patch of road ahead by the front wheel, but I heard his voice, looked up and there he was, stretched out and looking far too comfortable in the shade of a tree beside the road. It was the elderly gentleman of St Jean, the one with the boys.

'*Bonjour,*' he said again, nodding cheerfully.

'Er....' I croaked, '*Bonjour.*'

'*Vous allez a St Jacques?*'

'Er. . .*oui.*'

'*Moi aussi, avec ma femme et les gosses. Vous prenez un verre?*'

Jacques was from Pauillac, the wine country of the Medoc near Bordeaux and he had a well-chilled bottle of the real stuff tucked in the crook of his arm; a few glasses of that did wonders. As a bottle was emptied a squeal of brakes announced the arrival from above of a battered Citroën bearing further essential supplies and Isabelle, Jacques' wife. Hot on her heels, like fighters escorting a bomber, came *les*

gosses on their bicycles: Marin, Gabriel and Armand, their grand-children, all pilgrims to Compostela.

Armand later sent me a copy of the essay he wrote which describes our meeting: '*Sur le Chemin, Bon-Papa recontré un reporteur anglais, completement ecroulé. Il le remonté avec des biscuits trempé dans du vin.*

I am not quite sure about the *ecroulé*, which my dictionary defines as 'a state of collapse', but I will accept (and did accept) the biscuits soaked in wine. Jacques Viallard was seventy-two, a lawyer from the Medoc, now on his second trip to Compostela. On their previous journey, when Jacques was a youthful seventy and Isabelle in her late sixties, they had both ridden all the way from Bordeaux on bicycles, but now they were getting on a bit, Isabelle drove the car, found accommodation and passed the wine, while Jacques, stubborn to the end, rode his bike and only accepted a lift when forced to. He preferred to act as shepherd to the three boys, the twins Marin and Gabriel at fifteen, and bespectacled Armand, a year younger, who turned out to be the intellectual one among us, his nose ever stuck in a book. I took to the Viallards and they adopted me at once. You will hear more of them as we ride to St James.

'You will love the *Camino,*' Jacques went on dreamily. 'Such towns, such castles; the wines of Rioja . . . not to be compared with our Pauillac, of course, but still . . . . Léon, what a city, and Cebrero . . . . Rob, you must see Cebrero; but most of all you will enjoy the fellowship of the Road.'

'I would like to,' I told them, as we sat around on the grass, 'but where are our fellow pilgrims?' Apart from the odd rumour of a lady from Lyon, the Viallards were the first I had met.

'That's because you are far behind,' chipped in Marin. 'There are many pilgrims up above, at Ibañeta, and a friend of Bon-Papa is there, with the English tea.'

That settled it. We rose, Jacques to place his cycle on the car roof and ride up with Isabelle, the boys with their steel legs escorting me for a while until, unable to endure my plodding pace, they stamped on their pedals and raced off up the hill for the second time that day. If I covered a thousand miles on the Road to Compostela, they must have done twice that, riding to and fro, to urge me on, but then a French boy on a bicycle is not of this world.

Eventually, late in the afternoon and the ordeal of the hosre-flies stoically endured, the woods finally fell away. Mounting for the last slope (for I have my pride), the col of Ibañeta appeared. 'Rest' says a notice on the summit, 'Rest now, and hear the horn of Roland calling for his Emperor,' and I was glad to.

We rested on the grass beside the motor caravan from which Jacques' friend, another lawyer from Bordeaux, dispensed tea. Here Jacques presented me with a small pilgrim medal, like the ones he and the boys had hung round their necks, a small grey metal plaque, etched with the image of St James, produced by *Les Amis-de-St Jacques,* the French

confraternity of pilgrims.

'Wear that,' said Jacques, 'and people will help you on the Road, and other pilgrims will know who you are.' Within two day this prophecy turned out to be correct.

At last there were plenty of pilgrims. They swarmed here on the Ibañeta, examining the obelisk which marks the spot where Roland or *Rolden* fell in AD778, or simply inspecting their horse-fly bites. 'I thought bloodsuckers that big slept in coffins during the day,' one American remarked.

The Ibañeta col, which is also called the Port de Cize, is a fine spot, the crest of the watershed between France and Spain, with splendid views to the north, and a merciful breeze on this scorching day to blow at least some of the heat away. The footpath route from St Jean descends to this point, where the Road crosses the col, but the great monastery of Roncesvalles itself lies a mile to the south, sheltering below the crest. There was a church on Ibañeta once, but only the ruins remain of the one Charlemagne built in memory of his dead paladins. After a stroll about we packed up, mounted our bikes again and breezed down the winding road, rolling through the woods to the Abbey at Roncesvalles, into which we hurtled far too fast, just after the great church which holds the tomb of Sancho *'el Fuerte'*, 'Sancho the Strong, 'He of Las Navas', had closed for the day. We contented ourselves with a stroll around the cool cloisters, in some welcome shade from that still-scorching sun, but as we emerged, blinking, from the darkness, a girl came up and took me by the arm.

'Are you the man who is looking for me?' she asked.

'I am,' I admitted. 'And you are the lady from Lyon?'

And so she was.

*   *   *

When I had been enquiring for her in St Jean and Val Carlos, she had been wandering the woods near Ostabat, but I never did find out why Eve, the lady from Lyon, took the cockle-shell and set out on the Road to Compostela. Perhaps it was to shake off the after-effects of her divorce, perhaps to escape the attentions of her lover, the soulful Bruno, whose letters lay in ambush at every *post-restante*. She never said, and we didn't ask. Just twenty-six and very determined, Eve slipped easily into our little group.

'How much cycling had you done before you left Le Puy?' I asked her, as Jacques led his flock purposefully towards the bar.

'I had ridden the *vélo* home from the cycle shop,' said Eve, 'that's all.'

'And what did your family think about all this?'

'They thought I was mad,' That determined look, one that we got to know well, settled across her face. 'But I came anyway.'

Roncesvalles isn't the prettiest spot; the abbey is all gaunt grey buildings with corrugated roofs, but then it was built for utility, not beauty, to aid pilgrims struggling across the mountains. It was founded around 1130 by the Augustinian canons, before the Cluniacs tightened their grip on the Road.

The Abbey of Roncesvalles

It came under the direct protection of the Pope and attracted gifts from Augustinian communities as far away as Scotland. Pilgrims poured past here throughout the centuries and were provided with food and a bed for up to three days, treatment if they were ill, and a grave if they died. All we needed now was a drink, some food, a campsite, and a bath, and so, while the Viallards took off down the mountain into Spain, Eve and I pitched our tents by the river and joined the other pilgrims in attempting to dam the stream and make it deep enough to bathe in. Scores of tents lay along the banks and before long the occupants had created an adequate pond.

*   *   *

Next morning began with the rumour that ETA, the Basque terrorist organisation, had exploded a car bomb in Burguete, a few miles down the Road. The sun rose early and was already scorching through the trees as we packed up slowly and drank a little coffee, standing about in groups, and then set out to see the sights. Roncesvalles still functions as an abbey and, apart from the abbey church, contains a small museum and an even smaller ninth-century chapel of Santiago, our own St Jacques.

The abbey, much rebuilt and roofed with corrugated iron, is not very appealing, but it has been cleaned up in recent years and looked passable in the sunshine, while the chapel and tomb of Sancho VII, 'the Strong', is quite magnificent. Sancho led the Navarrese contingent to the battle of Las Navas de Toloso in 1212, when the Christian kingdoms finally combined to overthrow the Moors. Las Navas was the battle that finally turned the tide of the *Reconquista* and during it the Basques broke the Negro bodyguard of the Sultan Miramoulin, who had chained themselves together, and made a last stand about his tent. Parts of those chains still hang by El Fuerte's tomb, and the chains carved on the arms of Navarre recall that famous feat-of-arms.

The treasury contains various relics of Navarrese kingdoms, or even of Charlemagne, with war-clubs ascribed to Roland, but almost certainly much later; an emerald which belonged to Miramoulin; and various reliquaries, one of which contains part of the True Cross. I am not too fond of museums, especially when real live history is flowing past the door and, as the morning was advancing, it was time to leave. Eve decided to stay on and rest for a day and wait for the rest of her luggage, which her friend Jean, a cleric from Vannes, had offered to bring up from St-Jean-Pied-de-Port, so I left her by the abbey, and set off down the mountain for Pamplona.

*   *   *

I had better explain now about the heat. During the next few days Spain was to experience a heatwave beyond all recorded experience. I have the newspapers before me and they record the relentless rise in the thermometer to 40^{0}C (hottest for many years), to 43^{0}C (hottest in living memory), to 46^{0}C (hottest since records were kept). People keeled over, factories closed, work in the fields stopped. During all this, the pilgrims, facing the deadline of St James' Day, struggled on towards Compostela. Cycling, even downhill, in such heat is exactly like riding a blowtorch, but one of the problems with heat-exhaustion is that you tend to notice it long after you have passed the point of acting sensibly. I passed through Burguete where there were truckloads of Guardia but no signs of bomb damage, and rescued my cycle from a swarm of bees which settled on a branch of a tree it was leaning against.

Burguete ought to be a famous place; Hemingway came up here from Pamplona to fish and get drunk, and it became a popular haunt between the Wars for the American *literati* and besides, it's pretty. To hell with the *literati,* they only serve to put the price up. By the time I had reached Aioz at the foot of the mountain though, I was already in serious trouble. I fell into a bar and sat there clutching a *Fanta,* feeling crushed. That need to press on still had me in charge, so I went out into the mid-day heat and climbed again into the saddle. The metal of the bicycle, even after half-an-hour in the shade, was still too hot to touch, but slowly, very slowly, I pedalled on.

According to the map there are less than twenty fairly flat miles between Aioz and Las Campanas but it took me the rest of the day to get there and most of this distance passed in a daze. I remember getting off at one point and lying down on my spreadout map, which instantly disintegrated under the sweat. Running out of water, I scrabbled about for it in ditches. The day became one long search for shade, but there is little shade on the Road across Navarre and by mid-afternoon I had *had* it.

I was pushing the bike along the verge when I came to a farmhouse, and here at last some sense set in. There seemed to be no one around as I searched about slowly for a tap. I seemed unable to shout, but as I stood swaying in a downstairs room, there came a clattering from above and three sleepy-looking young men came tumbling down a ladder, *post-siesta,* and looked at me curiously. I simply held out the waterbottle. One took it and then caught sight of Jacques' pilgrim medallion which hung around my neck.

Larressingle

The Santa Maria Gate, Burgos

Castrojeriz

'Ah!' he said, turning to the others, 'he is a pilgrim to Santiago.'

Then I found out that Jacques was right about the kindness of the Road. They brought me a chair, a bottle of milk, well chilled from their fridge, which I clung to desperately, and offered me a bed in the corner if I wanted to stop the night.

'You are crazy to ride in this heat,' they told me urgently. 'Have you not seen the reports in the papers?' At that time I had not, and as I slowly recovered and the evening came on, with some slight diminution in the heat, I set off again. They watched me go as I wobbled away, shaking their heads and waving until I passed out of sight.

Having destroyed my map I did not even know where I was, but riding along brought me, by now exhausted once again, into the straggling hamlet at Las Campanas, a mixture of old houses and filling stations, south and east of Pamplona. After buying a new map, I fell off outside a small hotel beside the road, and lay there against the wall until rescued by the owner, who was himself a cyclist, and a typical hospitable Basque. Somehow all was taken care of and I lay, half-dead, in my darkened bedroom until the growing racket from the dining room below sent me down to see what the fuss was about. My host and his clientele, all in their San Firman costumes of white with red sashes, were winding themselves up for a night on the town, and I was dragged in to join the fun. A bottle or two later I felt practically human, and having acquired a red neckerchief and sash, looked almost one of the boys.

'Tomorrow,' cried the *patron,* pounding me on the back, 'we will go to the *encierro* at Pamplona, and run with the brave bulls.' With that cheerful prospect, I staggered upstairs and fell into bed.

Chapter 6
The Road to the Rioja

'If the future and the past really exist, where are they?

St Augustine

Seen from my window at dawn next morning, even the countryside appeared exhausted. A dull yellow light lay across the land, trees and telegraph poles sagged under the burden of another day. The only person in sight walked slowly, head bowed, across the stubble of a vast grainfield. I picked up my panniers and trudged downstairs in search of a quick coffee, intending to sneak off and avoid dicing with death in the streets of Pamplona, but I had no such luck.

The Basques were already up and drinking, greeting my arrival as a sign to be off; and my resolve wilted. I do not care for bullfights, and being chased through the street in the morning *encierro,* when the bulls are run from their pens to the ring, was one traveller's experience that I could do without. Hemingway has a lot to answer for though, so in the end we compromised. I would ride my bike to Eunate, the Basques would collect me from there and take me to Pamplona; after that, we would see. I downed my coffee and left, hurrying along empty roads, over nice flat countryside, to the church at Eunate which lies on the route from Jaca and is set in a grainfield beside the pilgrim road.

The building is Romanesque and quite beautiful with a rare exterior cloister which completely encircles the chapel, and shelters pilgrims from the heat or the rain. The door was firmly locked and I just had time to take some pictures and hide the bike behind one of the walls, before a hooting from the road announced the arrival of my companions.

That morning Pamplona resembled a battlefield. There were bodies everywhere. The San Firman festival is held each year from 6 to 20 July and celebrated with what the

Pilgrim church at Eunate

guidebook calls 'joyous ardour', a nice name for a two-week drinking session. The highlight of each day is the *encierro,* or 'running of the bulls', celebrated by Hemingway in his book *The Sun Also Rises* (or *Fiesta,* depending on your edition).

We hurried through the streets, stepping over the many victims of last night's orgy, and found the route of the *encierro* barred by a barricade and several Guardia who, curses, were impressed by my press-pass and let us through. We found ourselves in an empty street where the balconies were crowded with people all peering down the road to our right; somewhere a gun exploded, and the crowd shouted happily; somewhere close by the *encierro* had begun. I looked about for handy doorways and trees to climb.

We turned a corner to face a mob in white and red, running hard in our direction. Whatever was chasing them I could do without, so I turned and fled, legs wobbly, eyes on the lookout for a tree or a nice high grille. That is the last I saw of my companions. Basques raced past, yelling, waving rolled-up newspapers, then a clanging, then a bull — no, a steer — the bell clanking at its neck, cantered past. The numbers overtaking me accelerated, all looking back, and then a bull swept by, huge, black and shining, its horn-tips glinting sharply in the sun. The crowd above me roared. Close to, the bull appeared huge, implacable, impervious to the men running hard alongside. There must have been others, for there are six in each *encierro,* but I cannot recall them. Suddenly, we were in the bullring, the bulls had gone and the runners were strolling about yelling, waving up to the crowd in the stands, waiting for the next event. I climbed up on to the barrier to be hauled into the stand by a host of helpful arms, and sat down for a pant. The 'joyous ardour' continued all about, with wineskins passing from hand to hand, while a young bull with padded horns rushed about the ring below, knocking people down like ninepins. The Basques, who are gluttons for punishment, like to scrum down before the entrance to the ring, so that when the young bull rushes in to confront this human wall, it tries to jump and crashes headlong into it; the carnage was considerable. After ten minutes of this I left, thinking that if we must have towns full of drunks in this world then let them be Basques. Everyone was cheerful and unlike most mobs there was no sense of menace; no one was looking for trouble or out to have more than a good time.

*   *   *

Pamplona is the great city of Navarre and was once a major stop on the pilgrim road, supporting a large population of French who lived by assisting travellers on the *Camino Françes.* The hostel of San Miguel, next to the cathedral, had fifty beds for pilgrims and offered them bread, wine and a simple dish of meat and vegetables before departure, and there were many other such hostels dotted about the town. The cathedral stands by the river Arga, and claims, with some reason, to have the finest Gothic cloister in Europe. Those who diligently search the pavement in the Calle San Ignacio will find the spot where Ignatius Loyola, founder of the Jesuits and at the time an army officer, was wounded during the siege of Pamplona in 1521. Picaud, who divides the *Camino Françes* to Santiago from

Roncesvalles into thirteen stages, puts Pamplona at the end of
the second stage, which he describes as short, as is the next, a
bare 43km to Estella; even so, the sun was up and another hot
day was developing. I saw all I wanted of Pamplona early in
the morning as the crowds dispersed after the *encierro*. Then I
found a fairly sober taxi driver and bought my way back to
Eunate, feeling that yet another landmark in a travelling life
had been ticked off my list.

From Eunate the road was west across the golden grainfields
of Navarre, past Obanos on its hill and out to the junction with
the main road from Pamplona where all the pilgrim roads
finally come together, with still over 600km to go before
Compostela. The spot is marked with a bronze statue of a
pilgrim. From here there is only one *Camino de Santiago*, which
leads directly to the bridge at Puente la Reina. The old pilgrim
road leads down the Calle Mayor, past the Church of
Santiago, and out over the Arga. There is a modern bridge a
few hundred metres away, but even modern pilgrims cross by
this old one. It was built at the end of the eleventh century by
command of Queen Urraca, wife of Alfonso VI of Navarre, to

101

The old bridge at Puente la Reina

Pilgrim statue at Puente la Reina

ease the passage of travellers down the pilgrim road. Like Pamplona and many other towns along the Way, Puente la Reina had a French colony, and lying so close to the final junction of the various roads, was filled each summer with vast multitudes of pilgrims. I had a proper breakfast in a café by the bridge and wheeled my bicycle over, admiring the reflection of the bridge in the waters of the river below.

Crossing the Arga, the route swerves up to the village of Cirianqui, and them down to cross the Rio Salado where, according to Picaud, the Navarrese made a good living skinning horses poisoned by the waters. Cirianqui is a pretty little place, full of medieval houses, many bearing carved coats-of-arms, and from there the road drops down to the valley and presses on to Estella, and third stop on the Road across Spain as described by Picaud, who just for once, had something nice to say about a country outside his native Poitou: 'Here there is good bread, wine, meat and fish, and all manner of good things, the water of the river Ega is sweet, clean and good.' Estella is still a good place, green and shady, and home of *Los Amigos del Camino d'Estella*, who help travellers on the Road, as does the *patron* of the Residencia Tatan. Estella is full of churches, far too many to visit, so I settled for San Pedro de la Rua, which has a Mozarabic doorway and lies up a monstrous flight of steps just off the pilgrim road in the centre of the town, and a glimpse of the carvings on the twelfth-century Palace of the Kings of Navarre, one of which shows Roland jousting with the giant Faragat.

Estella is a pretty spot, truly *Estella La Bella*, and it being by now mid-day and blazing hot, I should have stopped there. Instead, I pressed on and by the time I reached the monastery at Irache, barely two miles outside the town, I was again flagging under the appalling heat. Fortunately I could take shelter in the church for a while and rightly so, for it was founded for pilgrims in 1051, but on the whole, that afternoon's ride, walk and crawl to Los Arcos, was another punishing journey. It is barely ten miles but it took me over four hours before I fell off my bicycle outside the Hotel Monaco and staggered into the bar.

The Monaco, inevitably, was full of Basques, the walking

wounded from the San Firman festival. Once I had recovered a little and they had discovered that I was English, they were, as ever, friendly and one went off '...to find one of your countrymen.' He turned out to be an Australian, or rather a Basque who had emigrated to Australia forty years before and returned for a final look at his native village, another endearing Basque character — but a little sad.

'I've been away... what?... over forty years, mostly in Queensland. It's funny to find your mates old men. I always thought of them as young blokes, like they were when I left... a lot of them are dead now. There was a lot of poverty here then, a lot of hunger....' We sat on for quite a while, swapping drinks, but his eyes looked past me, wide and full of the past.

I got to like Los Arcos. The locals were friendly, the beds comfortable, the food at the Monaco good and cheap. Best of all, it rained. First it thundered then it settled down to pour, the earth almost sizzling after those long, long days of heat. I went out to rescue my bicycle and dance in the rain and then I met Miguel and Santiago. Pilgrims to St James frequently sleep in churches and I found them sheltering in the doorway of the huge Church of the Assumption, a crumbling riot of Spanish Baroque, inspecting Santi's feet by torchlight. Santi's feet were in a terrible state. They were from Madrid, pilgrims to St James, and they had walked from Jaca. Miguel had survived the journey quite well but Santi was exhausted and in considerable pain. Miguel and I returned to the Monaco to pick up some beer and my first-aid kit.

'How long have his feet been like that?' I asked.

'Three or four days. We still have four hundred kilometres to go, so we have to keep going and do thirty kilometres a day — even more if we can. He wont't stop anyway.'

'But why not? It's pointless. His feet are practically raw. If they get septic....'

Miguel shrugged. 'His name is Santiago, and he wants to go to Compostela. He won't stop, so I just say nothing.'

We acquired bandages from the Basques and with that and my plasters did what we could for Santi's feet, and I left them to it in the great doorway of the church and went to bed. That

*The church at
Viana, where
Cesare Borgia
is buried*

night's rain did little to ease the heat, so I left early, just as dawn
was breaking, passing Miguel and Santi again without a word,
as they plodded grimly out of town, heads down, and rode on
as fast as I could to Viana, the last outpost of Navarre, and a
place I had long wanted to visit.

*　　*　　*

Viana lies on a hill beside a road, a dusty little place that
history has long ago passed by, yet here in 1513 Cesare Borgia,
who once held the world in his hands, died and is buried.
Cesare was the son of the Borgia Pope, Alexander VI, and is
usually presented as one of the great villains of history, the
archetype of Machiavelli's *The Prince*, supposedly the originator
of the autocratic belief that the end justifies the means.

Personally, I think he was much misjudged and like England's own Richard III, suffered in reputation after his death from chroniclers in the pay of his powerful and mean-spirited enemies, who pursued him beyond the grave. People who met him in his lifetime both liked and respected him. His castellans held his fortresses even after he was overthrown by Pope Julius and imprisoned, and Fleuranges, who served with him in the Italian Wars, refused to vilify his old comrade, saying simply, '...in war he was a kind companion and a brave man'. And here he lies at Viana, insulted even in death. Cesare was only thirty-two when he died, but in the course of his short but active life he became, for a short while, a cardinal, then left the Church to marry Charlotte d'Albret, sister to the King of Navarre, and a favourite of the Queen of France. Cesare became the Duke of Valence and in return for Papal favours was supplied with a French army, with which he conquered the rebellious towns of the Papal States. His aim, it would appear, was to stamp out all the despotic rulers of the peninsula , and unite Italy under the Pope.

All was going well for Cesare until his father died. All might still have been well, but, as Cesare told Machiavelli later, he had considered every possibility for when his father died, except the possibility that he might be ill himself. But he was, and before he could recover, his power had slipped away. Guillano Della Rovere, who hated all the Borgias, became Pope Julius II, so Cesare fled to Naples where he was promptly imprisoned by Gonzalvo de Cordoba, the Great Captain of the Catholic Kings, and shipped to Spain in chains. He eventually escaped from the fortress of Medina del Campo and made his way to the lands of his brother-in-law, the King of Navarre and, having failed to regain his dukedom in France — for all hands were now turned against him — he served in the king's army as a mercenary captain.

In 1513 the town of Viana was in rebellion, so Cesare, now Captain-General of Navarre, came to lay siege to it and soon had the town on the brink of surrender.

'Then the Lord Beaumont came by night to reprovision the fortress and this Borgia, ever mad for blood, hurried on his armour and rode out, spurring his horse into the press where, seeing him

Cesare Borgia's tombstone outside the church, so that passers-by would walk on his grave

alone, they enticed him into an *arroyo*, and beat him down and stripped him, and so he died, four men giving up their lives to the destruction of this bloody dog.'

'And the Pope was asked if a mass should celebrate the death of this villain, but His Holiness said that we should not give thanks for any man's death, but it seemed in truth to be a gallant feat of arms.'

'So this Duke died like a dog, and he whose motto had been *Aut Cesare, Aut Nihil*, was become nothing indeed, and of all his power and wealth and murders and treacheries, there was left nothing, save but a name to frighten children.'

Cesare was buried here, in the church of Santa Maria at Viana, but in the nineteenth century the local bishop, who must have had more vindictiveness than Christian charity, had the body removed from the nave and buried in the street outside the door, where all passers-by might step on it; and here he lies to this very day, under a simple paving stone marked *'Cesare Borgia, General of the Armies of Navarre, Gonfalonier and Captain General of the Holy Church'*. Well, he is beyond all praise or blame now, but he deserves something better than that.

*   *   *

I stayed up by the fountain close to Santa Maria in Viana for most of the day, draining and refilling my waterbottle frequently and set out for Logroño, now just five miles away across the burning plain in the late afternoon. After a mile though, I turned back. That fellowship of the Road that Jacques Viallard had talked about now had me in its grip. Somewhere back there, Miguel and Santi would still be coming on across the hills, thirsty, exhausted. I rode back and met them a few miles down the road, Miguel a good mile ahead of the staggering Santi. I circled round, removed the bottle from the carrier and waited for him to come up.

'I've brought you some water,' I said, holding it out and pressing it into his hand.

Miguel took a swig, then spat the water out upon the road. 'Ah, it's hot!'

'It can't be! I've just filled it from up there in Viana.'

'It's already hot. Never mind, it's water... good.'

'Drink that one, I'll take the other back to Santi.' I turned back towards the other figure shimmering in the heat rising off the road.

'He won't stop,' warned Miguel, as I rode off. 'If he does, he might not start again.'

Santi did not stop or speak, but he took the bottle and drank the water, limping along on those raw and blistered feet. The pain must have been terrible and I do not know how he did it. I do know *why*, though, for the Road to Compostela gets you like that. Months after I had returned home I met another pilgrim who told me of his own troubles on the Way and said, 'The Road has a way of finding you out; and then it's up to you to give in or fight the battle of yourself. After all, in theory you can always stop, but somehow once you get committed to the Road, you just can't.' Santi simply was not going to give in; there was something indomitable about him. The fact that to most 'sensible' people what he was doing was pointless was not the issue. He was going to walk to St James simply because he had decided to. I stayed with them throughout the rest of the afternoon, ferrying water to and fro from Viana, and we gathered up other pilgrims as we went, coming upon them one by one as they emerged from shelter. Eventually the sun gave up the struggle, letting us stumble at last into Logroño and the wine country of the Rioja.

Chapter 7
The Road across Castile

'Barons, mortgage your castles, demesnes,
towns or lands, but never give up war.'
Bertrand de Born

Logroño lies on the Ebro, that great river of Spain which flows right across the peninsula and eventually into the distant Mediterranean. It is also the capital of the Rioja wine country, a region which produces vintages said to be the finest in Spain. Seen from my tent at Camping la Playa on the far side of the river, Logroño looked attractive and a day in the city, strolling about, for a mid-morning coffee and a leisurely lunch, seemed a more attractive prospect than yet another punishing day on the Road. Miguel and Santi, the latter now in trainers and soft socks, set off at dawn but I awarded myself the day off. I also needed some running repairs to my bicycle.

Leaving all but my handlebar bag behind in my tent, I rode into town to find a bicycle shop. I stopped a passing cyclist who dismounted and led me to a workshop where one hard-pressed mechanic was working his way through a stack of dented machines. He shrugged his shoulders at my request for prompt assistance, and was turning away when my guide interrupted and caught him by the arm. 'You must help this man, and today,' he said. 'He is a pilgrim to Compostela.' The Road worked its magic yet again and inside half-an-hour I had a new spoke, a re-trued rear wheel and an all-round oil and polish. The price, and only because I insisted on paying, was 100 pesetas, about fifty pence. I began to like Logroño more and more, and it's a likeable place, with wide streets, shady boulevards and pavement cafés, the perfect kind of town.

The Road across the Rioja

The pilgrim traffic and the wines of Rioja developed together. The wine was first mentioned in 1102, although it was the Romans who brought the vines here centuries before that. Today wine is the principal local product and since the vintages of Rioja are improving steadily, Logroño is prosperous.

Pilgrims entered Logroño by the old bridge, the Puente de Piedra, past the Franciscan convent built to commemorate a miracle worked by Francis of Assisi when he made his pilgrimage to Compostela. The old road runs through the town, the Rua Vieja, the word *rua* inevitably signalling a place of passage for pilgrims. A few metres up this road lies a fountain, the *fuente de los peregrinos*, and just across the road the Church of Santiago el Real, which is noted for two statues of the saint, one showing him as a pilgrim, the other in his role as the patron saint of Spain, clad in armour, mounted on a most lifelike charger, and brandishing a sword. This is the other side of out saint, Santiago Matamoros, the 'Moor-Slayer', inspi-ration for the *Reconquista*.

The Moors entered Spain from Africa in the year 711, over-whelmed the Kingdom of the Visigoths, and rapidly overran the peninsula. Within a few years they had crossed the Pyrénées and showed every sign of conquering France until they were decisively defeated outside Poitiers by Charles Martel in 732. They withdrew below the Pyrénées, consolidated their conquest, and occupied much of Spain for the next 700 years. However, during that first invasion, when the bulk of the peninsula had been overrun, one small area managed to hold out, the Asturias and what is now Cantabrica, in the mountains of the Picos de Europa. Here the Moors experienced their first defeat in 722, at the hands of the half-legendary Pelayo, at the battle of Covadonga, the first step in the long road of the *Reconquista*.

The Moorish kingdoms of Spain were originally subject to the Caliph of Damascus but they soon established their independence. Cordoba became the capital of Moorish Spain, a famous centre for art and culture, producing architects, musicians and writers whose work influenced Christian Spain at the time and whose influence continues to this day.

The Moors were not the savage, warlike, uncultured infidels that history so often presents — quite the contrary. If anything, it was the Christian kingdoms of the North which produced the larger villains. Even the Eastern Crusades left a trail of devastation across Europe, from the Rhine to Constantinople, and achieved very little of consequence.

In Spain, the Christian and Moorish kingdoms were often at war, but more frequently at peace, quite prepared to trade together and they enjoyed long periods of truce and prosperity. Yet the pressure to expel the Moors from Spain was always there and only held in check by constant division among the Christian kingdoms. Then in 846, in the second year of the reign of Ramino II of Asturias, Santiago took a hand. The Asturians had long paid an annual tribute of one hundred virgins to the Caliph of Cordoba, but when Ramino came to the throne he refused to hand them over and gathered his army to meet the Moors on the plain below the castle at Clavijo. The battle raged all day, tens of thousands of men were locked in battle and the Christian side was falling back when, straight from the Heavens and leading an army of angels, came St James bearing his white banner marked with that red sword-shaped cross, rallying the Christians with his war-cry *'Santiago – y cierra Espana!'* 'St James — and close up Spain!'

Some say the saint killed 70,000 Moors at Clavijo, to gain his title of *Matamoros*, but who can say? The Moors were defeated, the virgins saved and Spain had a leader whose title no earthly kingdom dare dispute. Perhaps the battle at Clavijo never took place, for the history books make no mention of it until the eleventh century, but like many legends, it served a useful purpose at the time. The story of Clavijo established St James as the patron of Spain, secured the fortunes of his shrine at Compostela, and led to the pilgrimage which brought men, money and arms flooding south to aid the Christian kingdoms. Spanish knights were forbidden to serve in the Crusades to Outremer for they had work to do at home, and any Western knight could gain glory and Crusader indulgences by serving his time with the armies of Spain.

Many did so. Scots will recall how Sir James Douglas, bearing the heart of Robert the Bruce, fell fighting in Spain in the fourteenth century. Over a hundred years later, the English Lord Scales was wounded at the siege of Loja in Granada. Famous names are but the tip of the iceberg; throughout the *Reconquista*, St James, in person or through the force of his reputation, brought great assistance to the hard-pressed armies of the Lord.

Clavijo, where this famous encounter took place, lies only ten miles south of Logroño, and it looks like a good place for a battle. The castle on the hill was built to protect the road from the open plain of Castile, the *meseta* to the fertile Ebro valley. This country around Logroño has often been a battlefield, not least in 1367 when the English Edward of Woodstock, better known as the Black Prince, brought an Anglo-Gascon army over the Pyrénées to regain the crown of Castile for his ally Pedro the Cruel.

*   *   *

After a day in the shade, or swimming in the pool at La Playa,
I rode out in the evening, the cycle delightfully unladen, to
see the hill of Clavijo, and rose before dawn next day to beat
the heat on the next stage of my journey, to Najera. Pilgrims
had been filtering into the campsite all the time. Like me,
they were all on the move before daylight, striking their tents,
the sudden roar of a stove for a quick eye-opening cup of
coffee, a chink of metal as panniers were fitted to cycles. Then
we were all on the move, long lines filing through the still
sleeping tents, swinging into the saddle on the road by the
Ebro, and setting out to race the sun across Castile.

Apart from the problems of the sun, there was the heavy
traffic on the road that morning. Although most of the Road
to Compostela lies on very minor roads, this section from
Logroño to Navarette lies on a main route, and those heavy

trailer-tugging Spanish lorries made it a nightmare, bouncing across the road, hurtling past with a roar and a vast buffet from their slipstream. At Navarette the Road climbs off and over the main highway, presenting the brief and curious juxtaposition of a shepherd leading his flock of sheep along a dusty track as shepherds have done since time began.

I snatched some breakfast in the bus-station at Navarette, studiously ignored by drivers and passengers, the first intimation that this was Castile. Had they been Basques, a crowd would have collected to offer a *copa de vino*, and find out what I was at. The Castilians are not like that; who or what they do not know, they ignore.

The road out swerves round the hill called the Alto de San Anton, once fortified to provide the pilgrims with a hasty place to shelter if a party of Moors came galloping by, and

The Monastery of Santa Maria la Real, Najera

then past another height, the Puyo Roldan, Roland's Hill. The giant Farragut, a descendant of Goliath, had many Christian prisoners in his castle at Najera, and was guarding the gate when Roland threw a stone from this hill and laid him senseless — a fair throw of nearly two miles, but then Roland could do things like that.

Najera is an old town, crumbling attractively, with one great historic attraction, the Monastery of Santa Maria la Real, which was founded in 1032 when Najera was the capital of Navarre. It remained the capital until 1076 when Castile annexed the Rioja, but Santa Maria is the mausoleum of the Kings of Navarre, seven of whom lie in the pantheon, which is full of their marvellously decorated tombs. Here I found Miguel and Santi again, resting in the shade of the cloister.

'How goes it?'

'*Bastante bien.*'

Santi still looked terrible, but who was I to argue? I rode out to see the battlefield of Najera and then turned south for San Millan.

The battle at Najera took place during one of those pauses in the Hundred Years' War, and it is hard to see why the Black Prince chose to get involved in this Spanish quarrel, except to continue the Anglo-French Wars at one remove. Pedro the Cruel, King of Castile, was an unsavoury monarch, and when his bastard half-brother Henry of Trastamara overthrew him, everyone rejoiced. Pedro fled north, to the court of the Prince of Wales at Bordeaux in the duchy of Aquitaine, and in return for promises of commercial treaties, gained the assistance needed to regain his throne. The Black Prince was no lover of peace, and he sent for his captains and men-of-war.

Meanwhile, Henry of Trastamara, hearing of the storm gathering to the north, appealed for help to France, and the French king permitted his constable, the famous Breton knight, Bertrand du Guesclin, to raise an army from the free-companies of currently unemployed mercenaries then ravaging France, and lead them into Spain; apart from fighting the

English, itself a worthy cause, this also removed one problem from the soil of France.

It must have been a splendid sight, in the chill February of 1367, when the Anglo-Gascon army climbed the snowy passes to Roncesvalles and descended into Spain. 'Bitter cold it was,' says the Chandos Herald, 'sharp with wind and snow such that every man was dismayed.' All the great mercenary captains were there, Robert Knollys, Sir Thomas Felton, and old one-eyed John Chandos, now within three years of his death by the Vienne, and riding to his last great fight.

The first rounds went to the Spanish, who harrassed the English army, while letting disease do its work. The knights of Calatrava and Santiago, riding to join the king, surrounded Sir Thomas Felton's force of archers, which retreated to a hillside and fought to the last man, inflicting great loss on the Military Orders before they were overcome. The site of their stand is still known as *el alto de los Ingles*, the 'hill of the English'.

The main armies finally met on the banks of the Najerilla in April 1367. The Franco-Castilian forces were routed as they felt sharp arrows light amongst them. Their cavalry was flayed by the arrow-storm of the English archers, their foot soldiers hustled back to the riverside and slaughtered. It is said that the waters of the Najerilla turned red with blood and that bodies choked the river under the bridge at Najera. It was a famous victory but the victors got little good from it.

Bertrand du Guesclin was ransomed in the following year and raised another army to help Henry of Trastamara, who had escaped from the slaughter. Pedro went back on all his treaties with the Black Prince, who refused further assistance when Henry of Trastamara returned to Castile, Pedro was defeated and killed in 1369. All that the Black Prince got out of this campaign was his famous jewel, the Black Prince's Ruby, which now glows in the state crown and a fever, probably malaria, that weakened and finally killed him. Spain, they say, is a country where small armies are defeated, and large armies starve. The Prince's fine army was destroyed by 'the sickness of the host', or dysentery, and few returned to the north side of the Pyrénées.

From Najera the road runs south to San Millan, a place which I had it in mind to miss. One of the snags with cycle touring is that every mile costs effort. In a car a diversion of only ten miles is nothing, but on a bike that's a twenty-mile, two-hour, round trip, and you tend to think twice about it on the burning plains of Castile. Then I read Walter Starkie's comment that '... no true pilgrim could see St James and bypass his comrade in arms, St Millan', and as it was still early in the day, I turned my wheels south to the shrine of this other famous saint.

There are actually two monasteries at San Millan de la Cogolla, St Millan-of-the-Cowl; the upper one, called Suso, which dates from about AD1000, and the lower one, Yuso, deep in the valley, which is much later. San Millan died, aged 100, in 574, and his shrine soon became a pilgrim

The cloisters of Yuso Monastery, San Millan de la Cogolla

centre. Suso is set in a beautiful spot overlooking the Cardenas valley, and I prefer Suso to Yuso, which is too gilded and Baroque for my taste. Suso is a marvellous mixture of the Gothic, the Romanesque, the Mozarabic, and bit of this and a bit of that, which blends here into a marvellous, pleasing whole. One unforgettable sight is the now empty sarcophagus of St Millan. They say that when the saint's body was placed upon it, it melted into the stone, and when Garcia of Navarre tried to move the saint's body to a more profitable location in Najera, the coffin grew so heavy that no one could move it, which is all to the good, for this sarcophagus is a marvellous work of art. There is a full-sized effigy of the saint surrounded, as is his due, by 'weepers' or mourning figures, while at his feet stand other pilgrims, come to beg for help at the tomb of the saint. I saw the treasury at the Yuso monastery, which is now occupied by Augustine friars, and marvellous it is, but it is this tomb of St Millan which will draw me back to Suso.

North-west of San Millan lies the town of yet another famous saint of the *camino*, Saint Dominic, at Santo Domingo de la Calzada. I arrived there in the early afternoon, dismounted in the shade of the cathedral and looked up from chaining the

Cathedral at Santo Dominingo de la Calzada

wheel to see the Viallard family coming towards me across the square, beaming.

'We heard you were coming,' cried Marin, 'and you are staying with us at the Santa Teresita, with the nuns.'

'Am I?'

'Yes, and we must hurry back to lunch,' put in Armand, 'and Eve is coming too and will be here soon.'

You cannot be lost or lonely on the Road to Compostela. There is a certain pace you settle into, and it keeps you in touch with your friends as the pilgrims, flowing along, stopping to rest, passing and re-passing, talk to one another and pass messages along. By now I was 'our English journalist' to the Viallards and Eve was 'the lady from Lyon'. Like Miguel and Santi and the Viallards we were known to the pilgrims. It is usual to pass messages for faster travellers to carry forward, or stick notices on signs for the information of slower pilgrims; there was one in the cathedral doorway at Santo Domingo: 'Luis, we are here on the 11th. Meet us in Léon, six o'clock on the 20th, abrazos — Pepe.'

The hotel of the Santa Teresita is a curious place, half-hotel, half old folks' home, and run by nuns. They dash about in the full kit of gown and wimple, and all are equipped with bleepers, making it, as I said to Jacques, a great place to get a nun in a hurry. The nuns are also very efficient and hospitable, especially to the true pilgrims who, on production of their stamped passport, can get double portions at no extra charge. I parked my bicycle in the hall, was shown to my room, and was sitting on the bed writing up my notes when there was a tap on the door. There stood Eve and our little *confrèrie* from Roncesvalles was together once again.

Lunch at the Santa Teresita was a cheerful affair, full of chat about out adventures over the past week, interrupted only by the regular crash of breaking plates as the old folk further down the dining room dropped their dishes on the floor. Jacques also overplayed his hand by outlining his views on the role of women in modern society.

'A woman has three duties,' he declared, striking them off on his fingers. 'First, to please her man; second, to cook and clean; third, to have children.'

Isabelle, perfectly well aware where the power lay, *chez-elle*, looked philosophic, but Eve began to simmer like a boiler under full steam, so I took her off hurriedly to see the sights of the town. The camping-van of her friend at Roncesvalles, Jean, a cleric from the cathedral of Vannes, was parked in the main square, where we took a cup of coffee and discussed the famous legends of Santo Domingo.

Santo Domingo was an eleventh-century hermit who built a bridge across the nearby Oja, the river which gives a name to the wine, the Rio-Oja, or Rioja, and a causeway or *calzada* leading up to it to help pilgrims on the Road to Santiago. He also built a hospice by the Way and a small town soon grew up about it, Santo Domingo died in 1109 but his silver-plated tomb can still be seen in the part-Gothic, part-Romanesque cathedral in Santo Domingo, along with a cock and two hens which recall a strange event of the medieval pilgrimage.

The story is first told by Nompar, the Lord of Caumont, who made the pilgrimage in 1417. It appears that a young man passed this way on pilgrimage to Santiago, and caught the eye of a young lady at the inn. When he refused to stay with her she hid some silver in his scrip, and when he had gone, reported it as stolen to the authorities. The young man was hauled back, searched, tried and swiftly hanged. His heartbroken parents went on to St James, but when they returned some weeks later and passed by the gallows, the young man spoke, 'I am not dead; Saint James and his servants have preserved me alive. Go to the justice and bid him hie hither and let me down.'

The parents hurried to the magistrate and found him at supper, but when they told him the tale he was, not surprisingly, somewhat sceptical. 'If this tale be true,' he declared, 'these fowls on my dish would stand up and crow.' Which of course, they did!

This miracle, or rather miracles, caused quite a stir and in memory of the event a cock and two hens are kept in the cathedral of Santo Domingo to this very day. They live in a cage close to the tomb of the saint, and serve in shifts, like sentries, being replaced every few days from a small flock.

Pilgrims like to collect their feathers to put in their hats, and will feed crumbs to the birds. It is said that if the birds peck up the offering, the pilgrim will come safely to Compostela; if not, he or she will surely die along the way.

Eve, Jean and I went off to inspect the birds, and eventually persuaded them to cluck and crow, a strange sound to hear in a church, then wandered about the town which, after falling into ruin for several centuries, is now being gradually restored. The hostel built for pilgrims by Santo Domingo is now a *parador*, one of those marvellously appointed State-run hotels. I decided to stay there on the following night, for a little more rest and recreation, while Eve and the Viallards rode on to Burgos, a decision which involved me in a typically Spanish run-around.

The *parador* at Santo Domingo is a wonderful place, with comfortable rooms, an historic hall and dining room, good food and wine, but getting away can be a trial.

I clattered downstairs before eight next morning, eager to pay my bill and leave, to find the place empty except for an old porter washing the floor with a mop. After hovering about for a while I asked if I could pay him, so he put his mop and bucket away and, eventually, found my bill. This he added up, lips moving, then turned to me in doubt.

'This wine you had at dinner, Señor, what was it?'

'The house wine, *vino de mesa*.'

'Si, but what kind? *Quel marca?*'

'I don't know! The house plonk; whatever it is you serve here.'

Clearly, this would not do. He wanted the wine in detail with name, rank and number. We argued about this for a while as time ticked away, and then he came up with a solution.

'I will tell you what I'll do, Señor, since you are in a hurry. I will charge you for half-a-bottle of champagne. Then I cannot lose. That's the best way.'

This solution did not impress me. 'Not a chance. Look, a full bottle of Rioja red is only 400 pesetas, so I'm not paying 600 pesetas for half-a-bottle of the most expensive wine you have,

Crossing Castile

and the one I *know* I didn't drink. I'll pay you one hundred pesetas, which is probably too much. Take it or leave it.'

His eyes widened. 'But Señor, what are you saying? You cannot expect *me* to lose.'

I speculated on the sentence I might get for manual strangulation but violence was prevented by the arrival of last night's waitress, who sorted out the problem in a flash for fifty pesetas; smiles all round and hearty handshakes. The porter even came out into the square to wave me goodbye. They drive you frantic but you cannot help liking them.

*   *   *

The ride from Santo Domingo to Burgos is beautiful, perhaps the most attractive of the entire Way. The weather seemed cooler, for the heatwave had finally passed its peak, and the day began with a flat run across the plain of the Rio Oja, through the half-empty villages of Granon and Redecilla del Camino, where I filled my bottle at a wayside pump erected for pilgrims and marked with the cross of St James, and up to the high Montes del Oca, the Goose mountains, which bar the road to Burgos. After the heat, I felt strong and sailed up the mountain with ease, arriving at Valdefuentes in time to share a picnic lunch with a large group of Spanish, or rather Catalan pilgrims, marching from Barcelona. Ameri Picaud went a little north from here to San Juan de Ortega, which had another pilgrim hostel founded with the help of Santo Domingo in 1090. San Juan was buried here in 1163. The church and hostel still stand, quite empty on this hot afternoon, and the track that leads back to the main road is part of the old pilgrim route, and used for centuries by Compostela travellers. From here I rode west, swooping easily down the far side of the Montes del Oca and across the plain to Burgos and my next problem.

I checked into an hotel, was asked for my passport, and I could not find it! In all that fuss over the bill that morning, I had forgotten to ask for it. I beat my head against the wall, and went to the bus-station for another encounter with the Spanish temperament. Every bus route seems to be handled by a separate company, so it is first necessary to track down the right line and window and since no one is interested in helping a rival concern, this took time. When I finally found the right window, I had the following exchange with the man reading a newspaper behind the grill:

Me: A ticket for the six o'clock bus to Santo Domingo.
Him: (folding the paper) There is no bus today for Santo Domingo.
Me: (aghast) Are you sure?
Him: (smugly) Never on Sunday.
Me: Today is Saturday.
Him: (aghast) Are you sure?

Things like this also drive you frantic, but as I kept telling Eve, a lady who does not suffer fools gladly, '*Estamos en España*'. Not surprisingly the six o'clock bus was empty but it was much later that night by the time I had returned to Santo Domingo, collected my passport, and bumped once again across the mountains of Castile and wearily into bed at Burgos, the historic city of El Cid.

Chapter 8
The Road to Léon

'Thou shalt come out of the north parts, and
many people with thee, a great company and
mighty army.'

Ezekiel 38:15

Burgos is a very fine city. I could see that even as I manhandled
my bicycle down the steps of the hotel into the fresh-smelling
streets, full of smartly dressed people hurrying to work. The air
was crisp, cool and springlike, very refreshing after the heat of
the last week and surprising too, though they say that in Burgos
summer begins on the day of St James, 25 July, and ends on
that of St Ann, 26 July. Riding down towards the old city gate
by the Arlamzon to where the filigree spires of the cathedral
were poking holes in the sky, Burgos seemed a very good place
to be, and my small sense-of-humour crisis of yesterday was
already a thing of the past.

The Santiago pilgrim has three sights to see in this city; the
monastery of Miraflores, the convent of Las Huelgas, and the
great Gothic cathedral of Santa Maria; all have some
relevance to the Compostela pilgrim, but only in passing, for
Burgos, is above all, the city of El Cid.

Rodrigo Diez de Vivar, known to history as El Cid, the
Campeador, or champion of Spain, was born in Vivar, a small
village a few miles outside the city. He is represented in that
epic poem *El Cantar de Mio Cid* as a great hero, a knight of
undentable virtue and a great warrior of the *Reconquista*, but
the reality is a little different. Rodrigo was a mercenary
captain, but one not without honour. He was born about
1045, into an age of considerable tribulation among the
Christian kingdoms, and just before the Moors made another
attempt to reconquer the peninsula. At the time of his birth,
Ferdinand of Castile had united his realm with that of Léon
and the Asturias, but on his death he divided up these

City gate, Burgos

kingdoms among his three sons, who promptly went to war
with each other. Garcia, the youngest, was soon eliminated
from the contest, but Sancho and Alphonso's wars tore the
Christian kingdoms apart. Untangling the wars of Spain is
always difficult, for the various kings shared a very limited
variety of names; Sanchos, Alphonsos and Ferdinands
abound, and sorting out which is which can be a problem.
Rodrigo served first the then King of Castile, Sancho II, then
his brother Alphonso VI of Léon, after Sancho mysteriously
died, supposedly murdered at Alphonso's instigation. Rodrigo
persuaded the king to declare publicly that he had no hand in
his brother's death and though the king reluctantly complied,
he then drove Rodrigo into exile where he took service with
the Moorish Emir of Saragossa. It was here that he became
known as El Cid from the Arabic *sidi*, the Lord. Rodrigo

125

hired out his sword and his *mesnie* to the highest bidder, and made war on Moor or Christian with complete impartiality. He laid waste the Christian Rioja and destroyed Logroño; in 1094 he captured the Moorish city of Valencia, where he ruled until his death in 1099, defending it against the latest tidal wave of Muslim invaders from Africa, the Almoravides.

By the mid-eleventh century, the Christians of Spain and the Moors of Al-Andaluz had learned to live together, and periodic wars were interspersed with long periods of peace and co-operation. This happy state of affairs was anathema to the fanatical Muslims of the desert chief, Yusef Ibn Tashafin, who landed at Algeciras in 1086, with a vast and well-equipped army. In October he defeated Alphonso at the battle of Sagrajas, near Badajoz, and rolled the Christian frontiers back towards the north.

Rodrigo, still out of favour with the king, was not present at Sagrajas, and the rest of his life was spent either beating back the Almoravides or attempting to placate his ever-distrustful sovereign. Burgos was the scene of many of his exploits, and the city contains many memorials to events in the life of the hero.

In the cathedral museum at Burgos stands an oak coffer which, so legend has it, the Cid, in great need of money, filled with sand and pledged to the Jews, swearing it was full of gold-dust. Trusting the word of the hero, they did not look inside. Rodrigo is buried in the cathedral beside his wife, the beautiful Ximene, and it was on the steps of the cathedral that he extracted the famous oath from King Alphonso, forcing the king to publicly swear three times his innocence of any involvement in his mother's death.

> 'Do you swear you had no hand in King Sancho's death?'
> 'I so swear.'
> 'Do you swear you did not counsel King Sancho's death?'
> 'I so swear.'
> 'Do you swear you did not conspire to cause King Sancho's death?'
> 'You try me too far, Rodrigo!'
> 'Swear it!'

El Cid shares many of the attributes of Roland. He had a

famous sword, Tizon, a favourite warhorse, Babiaca, which bore the hero's dead body, strapped in the saddle, on one last charge against the Moors outside Valencia, and his story seems half-fact, half-legend. There seems to be no truth in the story that he killed Ximene's father, Diego of Oviedo, the Champion of Castile, and indeed some Spanish scholars insist that he never lived at all, although this seems unlikely. Like St James, his life and legend were an inspiration for the *Reconquista* and pilgrims carried the news of his death back down the Road. 'Away in Spain, in Valencia, Don Rodrigo has died, to the grief of Christendom and the joy of the pagan' wrote a French monk in 1099, but the legend of the Cid, preserved in plays, in ballets, even in an epic film, still lives on.

Well, here he lies in Burgos and his wife beside him. As he is still the great warrior hero of Spain, who could pass this way and not pause to remember the one who was, in his day, the most famous knight in Christendom, even if the cathedral custodians will let you. I was taken to task by one of the guides for wearing a badge of my own coat-of-arms in a place devoted to El Cid.

That apart, and though I could easily suffer from cathedral fatigue, Santa Maria de Burgos is beautiful. It was built from about 1221, under the direction of the then-bishop of Burgos, Maurice the Englishman, who summoned masons from France to create a building which is a fine example of the Gothic. There is an effigy of Bishop Maurice in the transept, close to the tomb of El Cid, but my favourite place in the cathedral is the Constable's Chapel, which contains the tombs and effigies of Hernandez de Velasco, Constable of Castile to the Catholic Kings, and his wife, who lie together in creamy Carrara marble. A small lapdog nestles in the folds of the lady's gown, a nice touch. Less to my taste, in the Chapel of the Holy Christ, hangs the crucifix on which the figure of Jesus is covered in skin, not human skin as was once believed, but that of a buffalo; even so, it looks all to lifelike.

The Monastery of Miraflores, two miles to the east of the city, is another surprise, for although the exterior is drab and decayed, the interior is glorious. This is one of the mausoleums of the later Castilian kings, and their funerary chapel contains splendid effigies, rich scrolls and many coats-of-arms. Miraflores dates from the mid-fifteenth century, so the architectural style is Flamboyant Gothic but the Abbey at Las Huelgas, to the west of the city, is much earlier, mostly Romanesque and far more evocative of the pilgrimage.

Pilgrims were there on this bright morning, rolling up their tents after a night spent in the shelter of the walls, for as usual, any pilgrim church will help travellers to St James. Inside the cloister, and even more delightful, a service was in progress. A choir was intoning some Gregorian chant, which seemed just right in this setting, the voices echoing around the cloister and alon the dim corridors and chapels. Las Huelgas was Cistercian, though the abbey was originally built as the king's summer palace and it was Eleanor, daughter of Henry II of England and wife of Alphonso VIII, who gave it to the

Road through the ruins of the Convent of St Anthony, near Hontanas

French pilgrims at Leon

The old pilgrim road near Astorga

The castle, Villafranca

Church. Two attractions here for the pilgrim are the standards captured from the Moors at Las Navas de Toloso and in a room off the cloister, a medieval statue of Santiago Matamoros, fitted with articulated arms, which dubbed members of the royal family as knights.

*   *   *

The road from Burgos leads to the *meseta*, that flat windswept plateau which occupies so much of Old Castile. Since the country is fairly flat, the journey is easy, except for that prevailing and relentless westerly wind which holds the traveller back, and can get very wearing as the days pass. There is nothing to be done about this wind except change to a lower gear, crouch low over the handlebars and plod steadily into it, along a road dotted with ever-more frequent groups of pilgrims all forging west into the sun. Many of the villages on the Way, like Rabe de las Calzadas and Hornillos del Camino, have suffixes which reveal their long connection with the pilgrimage, and beside the road stand many crosses and fountains marked with the dagger-cross of Santiago. A little after Hontanas the Way actually runs through the ruins of the Convent of St Anthony, which straddle the road and date from the fifteenth century, while a mile further on a turn in the path reveals one of the most memorable vistas on the Road, the high bare hill crowned with the fortress of Castrojeriz. The village of Castrojeriz huddles at the foot of the hill, a quiet, sheltered sort of place, full of dilapidated medieval houses, many of them former pilgrim hostels, and here, riding their cycles round the old monasteries, were the Viallards once again. We took lunch together in a fly-filled café, dominated as always in Spain, by a television set going full blast in the top right-hand corner, and discussed the fact that Eve had disappeared.

'She went off yesterday on her own, over the *meseta*. She'll end up dead in a ditch,' grumbled Jacques. 'It's not safe for a girl on her own.'

Isabelle and I felt that unlikely. 'That girl can look after

129

Romanesque Church of St Martin, Fromista

herself,' said Isabelle decidedly, while I thought that any
man foolish enough to trifle with Eve in one of her
determined moods would be lucky to escape with his life.

'Anyway, she said she would see us all at Cebrero on
Friday night,' put in Armand, who was now on his third
greasy *tortilla castellaño*. 'You will have to hurry, we still have
a long way to go.'

The Viallards were staying on in Castrojeriz, but I decided
to press on to Itero and Boadilla del Camino, then on to the
Canal de Castile, where I rode along the towpath for a mile or
so into the town of Fromista. Fromista is a pretty little town,
built in a circle like a French *bastide*, and contains as a central
gem the golden-stone Romanesque Church of St Martin
which, quite rightly, is one of the national monuments of
Spain. It was founded in 1035 by Queen Dona of Navarre,
and 1188 passed into the hands of the Cluniac community of
Carrion de los Condes. It remains a parish church of the early

Middle Ages, still in beautiful condition and a real gem. There is a statue of St James in the nave, and light pours in from above to illuminate the golden interior.

I was taking a photograph or two of this marvellous building from across the street by the Hostal San Telino, when another cycle-tourist appeared, and obligingly agreed to circle the church a few times and add a little detail to the shot. This was Hank van Henk from the Hague, cycle-pilgrim to Compostela, and cycle-tourist *extraordinaire*. When Hank travels by bike, he goes the distance.

'Last year I rode from Holland to Aswan on the Nile,' he recalled over lunch. 'It took four months — I broke seventeen spokes.'

This year Hank was going across Europe like the wind, having reached Fromista in five days from Loire, '...and after Santiago I'll go on to Lisbon to meet my wife.' So saying, he climbed back into the saddle, went down through the gears and raced off across the *meseta*, and out of sight.

*　　*　　*

After Fromista, the *meseta* becomes an open, rather barren, desolate place. Eagles rove about the clear blue sky above the burnt grass, and grainfields reach to the horizon. In the village the main sign of life is the storks, shifting about on their tumbled nests high on the belfries. I am a desert-lover, so I like this open heartland of Castile. I began to stop in every village, to sit in the café, drink beer and inspect the locals who returned my gaze with reserved but intense curiosity.

The various peoples of the old kingdoms of Spain are very different from each other, and on a cycle ride you have time to notice it. The Basques are very outgoing, spontaneous, quick to recruit a stranger to their table. The Castilians tend rather more towards the popular idea of the Spaniard, silent, reserved but quite friendly in their own way. I would walk into a bar seeking a beer and a refill for my waterbottle and a silence would fall briefly over the customers. The barman would stand four-square in front of me, hands on the counter, and listen to my requests without expression. All were perfectly amiable and ten minutes later, when I left, they would come out to wave me goodbye. Later on, the Galicians appeared different yet again, more preoccupied with their cattle than the passing stranger, yet quick to offer a glass of wine or wave you into their houses for a rest.

After Fromista comes Villalcazar de Sirga, which was once famous for the White Virgin in the Church of Santa Maria which belonged to the Templars. I stopped again here, to lunch at El Meson, for Senor Pablo of El Meson which lies just opposite the church is a friend of Santiago and gives a great welcome to pilgrims travelling on foot or cycle.

Carrion de los Condes is much larger, and contains, apart from a story of El Cid, the relics of another saint, St Zoyle, which Fernando, Count of Carrion in 1047, obtained as tribute from the Emir of Cordova. 'Gold and silver I have in plenty,' he said. 'Give me the relics of St Zoyle.'

Given the trade that came with pilgrims to the shrine, his choice was profitable, but his sons fell foul of the Cid, by first marrying the Cid's twin daughters to get their hands on the Cid's dowries, and then ill-treating them. The Cid led his *mesnada* to Carrion, rescued his daughters and killed their husbands, later marrying the girls to princes of the House of Castile.

Today Carrion is a large town for the *meseta*. The Monastery of St Zoyle, now a pilgrim hostel where they stamped my *peregrinero*, is another national monument. There is also a fine church, Santa Maria del Camino, and a Temple de Santiago, as well as many medieval houses; Carrion de los Condes is a place to enjoy, and even Picaud favoured it, 'A fine rich town, full of wine, bread, meat and all good things.' Pablo Payo of the Meson Pisarrosas is another Amigo de Santiago, and welcomes true pilgrims to his bar.

After Carrion the Road heads west, across ever more desolate countryside, but edges north towards Léon to the pilgrim church at Las Tiendas, Terradillos de los Templarios, and San Nicolas del Real Camino, on the border between the provinces of Palencia and Léon. Then after a few miles into

The author and Eve, 'the Lady from Lyon'

the town of Sahagun which, according to Picaud was the seventh stop on the Camino in Spain. Sahagun is therefore full of pilgrim hostels and churches, all with Mozarabic elements, but most of them in ruins, especially the Convent of La Peregrina, which stands, shattered and empty, on a hill to the south of the town. Sahagun was a great centre for Mudejar craftsmen and the churches of San Lorenzo and San Tieso are both in this style.

West of Sahagun, the Road divides. While the modern metalled *carratera* goes one way the ancient pilgrim track splits into two, the *Calzada de los Peregrinos*, which follows a Roman road, the *via Trajana*, Trajan's Way, to Mansilla de las Mulas; and the more rugged *Real Camino Frances*, which leads to the same place but through Bercianos, El Burgo and Reliegas, all small, sunbeaten, tumbledown places. I followed the former, which stays close to the railway line, and it brought me to Calzadilla de los Hermanillos, a curious little place full of troglodyte dwellings. These are not uncommon on the bleak *meseta* and I originally thought that they were stables or cellars until I met an inhabitant and was invited inside for a look. The cave dwellings are hollowed out of the earth, and this one was vast, cool and comfortable, if a little dark. 'It's very practical,' the owner explained. 'Cool in summer, warm in winter, and if I want to make it bigger — I dig.'

The above-ground dwellings hereabouts are in adobe, so that the villages have a faintly Mexican air, until this track comes out into the main road at the walled medieval town of Mansilla de las Mulas, on the banks of the Rio Esla. The walls run along the southern bank of the river which acts as the moat, and the freshly-caught trout in Las Asturianos are delicious. From here the ancient pilgrim road follows the main route directly north to Léon, to Puente Villarente on the rio Porma, then Valdelafuente and so, after a long day in the saddle, to the splendid city of Léon, for a little more rest and recreation at the ancient pilgrim hostel of the Hotel San Marcos.

Hotel San Marcos, Léon

The San Marcos is one of the great hotels of the world. It was built as a pilgrim hostel by the Knights of Santiago and still bears the scallop-shells of St James on the outer walls and the red crosses of the Order of Santiago on the ceiling bosses in the cloister. Not surprisingly, the management and staff of the San Marcos are well used to pilgrims, even scruffy ones on bicycles. The doorman touched his cap and opened the door wide. No-one batted an eyelid as I wheeled the bike up to the reception desk, a click of the fingers summoned porters to wheel the machine away and carry my panniers to the bedroom, and ten minutes later I was deep in a hot bath.

The San Marcos was built around 1170 as the mother house of the Order of Santiago, although most of the present building dates from the late fifteenth century. Today it falls into three parts, the luxury hotel, which has a well-concealed modern extension, a small museum which is separated from

Cathedral doorway, Léon

the hotel lounge only by a glass screen, and the church. You need to use your eyes at the San Marcos to note the carved ceiling in the lounge, the exquisite little twelfth-century carving of the Christ of Carrizo in the museum, those ceiling bosses of Santiago in the cloisters, and much more.

During the *Reconquista* four Military Orders were founded in Spain; the Order of Calatrava, founded in 1158; Alcantara, founded in 1218; Santiago, founded about 1175; and much later, the Order of Montesa. All had as one tenet of their Rule the task of 'defending Spain from the enemies of the Cross of Christ'. The Order of Santiago was particularly devoted to the Road and took as its emblem a sword-shaped red cross on the white scallop-shell of St James. Their motto was *Rubet Ensis Sanguine Arabum*, 'Red is the sword with the blood of Islam' and over the long years of the *Reconquista*, the Knights of Santiago gradually gained ascendancy over the other Military Orders.

The Orders received support in terms of money from the Church, but their lands came from the king, and the lands he offered were usually those occupied by the Muslims. If the knights wanted possession of their lands they had to fight for it, a good way of extending the Christian kingdoms. Even today, a host of villages in Spain are suffixed 'de Calatrava' or 'd'Alcantara' as a reminder of those knights who took them from the grasp of the Moor.

After the fall of Granada signalled the end of the *Reconquista*, the purpose of the orders was accomplished. The Masterships of Calatrava and Santiago were incorporated into the Crown when King Ferdinand was elected as the last Master of Santiago. The Cross of Santiago became the mark of a servant of the Royal Household and can be seen in portraits by Velasquez or, even today, on the vestments of the priests in the cathedral at Compostela.

The size and beauty of the Hotel San Marcos gives some idea of the wealth and power of the Order in its heyday, and it is a splendid place to stay in while exploring the other two famous sights of this city, the cathedral and the basilica of San-Isidro.

Léon has had a troubled past, frequently besieged by the

rival Christian Kings and sacked by Almanzor on his march to Compostela, but the glories which remain are quite outstanding.

San Isidro is Romanesque and contains the relics of the saint who was Bishop of Seville. His body was translated here before Seville fell to the Moors, and the present church dates from the eleventh and twelfth centuries; it serves as the pantheon of the royal houses of Léon, Asturias and (yet again) Castile. This pantheon is well worth a visit, with splendid frescoes and carvings in the Romanesque crypt of the basilica. The treasury contains medieval caskets, jewelled cups and enamelware from Limoges.

I emerged from all this, blinking in the sudden daylight, to fall headlong over a doglead, held by one of two dusty, peeling-nosed French girls sitting on rucksacks bearing the *coquille de St Jacques*. They had walked all the way from Paris

Street market, Léon

with the dog, a pleasant mongrel.

'There are three of us,' one explained, 'and our *Prof*, from the Sorbonne. The others are inside looking at San Isidro. It takes us ages to see anything on the Way, as one of us has to stay with the dog, and go in afterwards.' The dog smiled and wagged its tail happily in the dust.

Léon swarmed with pilgrims that afternoon, their cycles and rucksacks piled up everywhere. There were more French students there, all tricked out in pilgrim gowns which turned out, on closer inspection, to be Moroccan *djbellas*, worn, I suspect, for effect. I took their photograph and met another pilgrim bearing a message from Eve. 'She passed me two days ago, and will meet you at Cebrero.' And then, dodging through the throng, came the Viallards, my *confrères*, ready to see the cathedral and take tea at the San Marcos.

The cathedral of Léon is one of the glories of Spain. It was begun in 1205 and is pure Gothic; the main door is beautifully carved, the stone soars and then there is the glass. There are 182 stained glass windows in Léon Cathedral, so many that their extent actually weakens the walls. Stand inside this cathedral, as we did, on a sunny afternoon and the effect is exactly like standing inside a kaleidoscope — the very air glows with colour. I am not often left breathless, but I was dazed by the beauty of Léon cathedral. We wandered round the walls and back to the San Marcos, our heads full of that Gothic wonder in glass and stone. Pilgrims, if you come this way, take time for the city of Léon.

Chapter 9
The Road to Santiago

'Though with great difficulty I am got hither,
yet now I do not repent me of the trouble I
have been at to arrive where I am. My sword I
give to him that shall succeed me in my
pilgrimage....and so he passed over, and the
trumpets sounded for him on the other side.'

John Bunyan: *A Pilgrim's Progress*

Some way west of Léon the *meseta* ends. Determined to catch
the Viallards and meet Eve again at El Cebrero, I left the San
Marcos early and raced away through the dawn across the
Bernesga, down a road lined with villages all partly *el Camino*,
through Trobajo del Camino, past La Virgen del Camino,
which was once a pilgrim sanctuary, until, after an hour-and-
a-half in the saddle, I rolled over the Rio Orbigo and got off
in search of breakfast.

There is a modern road bridge here at Hospital de Orbigo,
but the main interest centres on the Puente del Paso Honroso,
the 'Bridge of the Passage of Arms', a few hundred metres to
the north. In the Holy Year of 1434, a Spanish knight, Don
Suero de Quinoñes, held this bridge with nine companions
against all comers for thirty days. All gentlemen of coat
armour were obliged to joust before they could cross, and it
must have caused one of the greatest traffic jams of the
medieval world. It must also have driven many knightly
pilgrims to distraction; they had come all this way, and now
some local hero was trying to make trouble!

The *Paso Honroso* was one of the last romantic acts of the then
dying age of chivalry, and Don Suero, the last of the knights-
errant. He and his companions held the bridge for 'the honour
of St James and our ladies' and they ran over three hundred
courses in those thirty days, breaking every lance they had.
One knight was killed in the joust, and many were injured.

The fame of the encounter spread through the princely courts of Europe and a century later the exploits of Don Suero are credited with inspiring Cervantes to write *Don Quixote*. It also led to the death of Don Suero, for one knight, Gutierre de Quijada, unhorsed by Don Suero, harboured a grudge for his defeat and killed him twenty-four years later in a field near Castroverde in Navarre.

I ate my breakfast, the inevitable rolls and coffee, in the restaurant by the modern bridge, in some awe of a Spanish lorry driver wolfing down a vast fried breakfast at a nearby table, with the aid of a bottle of Rioja. The sight made me feel quite ill.

Hospital de Orbigo is a rather ramshackle place today, but it must have looked splendid during the days of the *Paso Honroso*; the tents and banners of the knights, the cheerful crowds, the cheers when another champion arrived, the roar of applause when yet another challenger was defeated. A stone pillar on the old bridge records the exploits of Don Suero and his companions, but of the old pilgrim hostel which once gave this place a name, nothing remains but ruins. It was nice to feel fit and strong and I made good time along the Road until I arrived at Astorga, another major spot on the Way.

At this point the pilgrim has a choice of two routes across the next major obstacle, the rugged mountains of Léon which bar

The Road through Orbigo

the frontier to Galicia. Astorga was once a Roman town; today it is a great centre for fairs, and capital of the country of the Maragatos, a tribe (or race) who are said to be directly descended from the Goths. They supported the Moors during the *Reconquista,* which was a decided disadvantage when the Christians triumphed, and they continue to wear their own distinctive costume of slouch hat, tight leather jacket and billowing pantaloons, at least on Sundays or to weddings or fiestas. There were no Maragatos about in Astorga on this busy workaday morning, so I made my way to the cathedral which, having seen the splendid Gothic church at Léon, I managed to avoid visiting, and passed on instead to the Museo del Camino, museum of the Road, in the archbishop's former palace.

The palace itself is a fantastical creation designed by the Catalan architect Gaudi, and looks very odd indeed, the sort of building which would slip easily into Walt Disney's *Magic Kingdom* rather than the medieval setting of Astorga, but I rather like it. It now contains a marvellous museum for pilgrims with a unique collection of photographs, maps, documents and sculpture relating to the *Camino-Frances.* I spent a very contented hour in here looking around the exhibits, wallowing in the story of the Road.

*   *   *

Astorga owes much of its past and present prosperity to its role as a road junction. Apart from the Road to Compostela, the *Via de la Plata,* the 'Silver Road' north from Seville terminated here and, until recently, all travellers to the north-west coast of Spain, to Coruña and Oviedo, passed this way. The English soldier, Sir John Moore led his army through here in full retreat before his death at Coruña during the Peninsular War in 1809, losing many of his men to less famous graves in the high, hard mountains of Léon and Galicia which still lie ahead.

Oviedo too had its place on the pilgrim road, and held itself out as a rival to Compostela.

*The Cruz de
Ferro*

*Quien va a Santiago
Y no a Salvador
Sirve al criado
Y deja al senor*

Or, to put it in English, he who visits Compostela and not Oviedo, serves the maid and not the master; the 'master' in Oviedo being the *Camara Santa*, the holy ark, which contains relics of the apostles in the Chapel of St Mark inside the cathedral. Many pilgrims still divert through Oviedo either on their way out or home, if only to see this fine city of the Asturias.

For those heading directly for Compostela there are two passes through the *Montes de Léon*, one through the pass of Manzanal, the other through Foncebadon and Monte Irago. The Mazanal route is the one followed by the main road, now being developed into an autoroute. The one via Foncebadon is not even shown on many maps, but that is the one featured by Ameri Picaud and therefore that is the one I took. It begins with a comforting flat stretch from Astorga, over the last of the *meseta,* and runs through a number of villages of the

Maragateria, the country of the Maragatos, before reaching El Ganso and starting to climb up to the village of Rabanal del Camino, the ninth stop on Picaud's route, a place full of familiar pilgrim signs; the old hostel, La Casa de las Cuatro Esquinas, the 'House of the Four Corners', the pilgrim fountain, the usual dusty church. Further on, a mile or so past Rabanal, there is another fountain, at Fuente del Peregrino, and the road climbs steeply past the abandoned village of Foncebadon to the Cruz de Ferro, on the top of the Montes de Léon, at 1504m (4,500ft), a high, windy and evocative spot for the pilgrims. The countryside was full of them, bright little dots, plodding west across the golden land.

The Cruz de Ferro, the iron pilgrim cross, juts out of a huge, high pile of stones, a *montjoie*. *Purchas his Pilgrim* noted that once upon a time there was a 'way that marked with *montjoie* from out of Englande to Saynt Jamez in Galise'. If so, very few remain and this is the only one found on my journey along the Road to Compostela. A *montjoie* is simply a cairn, but it was the

Road sign at El Acebo

143

custom of the Normans, and therefore probably of the Vikings, to pile up stones, or more likely the shields of their fallen enemies after a battle so that their leader could climb on it and be acclaimed by his victorious followers. William the Conqueror's men built a *montjoie* after their victory at Hastings and the English children's game of 'King of the Castle' is said to have its origins in this ancient custom.

It is still the custom for pilgrims to carry a stone to the *montjoie* above Foncebadon, and so I duly found one and clambered up to place it on the top, looking back just in time to see my own *confrèrie,* the Viallards, come cranking round the corner; more delights and more stones were added to the vast number piled about the Cruz de Ferro.

Two Dutch pilgrims came up to share our picnic lunch at Foncebadon and then we pressed on, down the western slopes of the *Montes de Léon,* out of the Maragateria into a green country of the Bierzo, and through the half-ruined village of El Acebo. The road is so bad here that even cyclists have to dismount. It seems strange to find places like El Acebo still existing in Europe in the last quarter of the twentieth century, but there it is; probably very little changed since Moore's

Road through El Acebo

Early morning at El Cebrero

Palloza (stone barn used by pilgrims) at El Cebrero

The monastery, Samos
Folk dancing at Santiago de Compostela, during the Feast of St James

defeated little army trailed through here nearly two hundred years ago. The road improves on the far side and falls away swiftly to Riego de Ambros, and Moulinaseca, where we arrived in the late afternoon, a loud ping from my cycle wheel announcing the end of yet another spoke.

With less than 200km still to go before Santiago, the foot pilgrims multiplied. Scores of them were paddling in the river or sheltering from the late sun beneath the arches of the bridge, and just outside on the road to Pontferrada, a large company of pilgrims appeared, having marched from Léon behind the banner of the local confraternity. Such groups appeared ever more frequently in the next few days, Scouts, youth groups, parties of friends, all pressing hard to the west as the city and the day of St James grew nearer.

Somewhere in the foothills near Pontferrada I lost the Viallards once again, and since I had done quite enough for

Pilgrims resting at Moulinaseca

Templar castle at Pontferrada

one day, I pulled off the road for the night, camped by the river, and spent the evening strolling about the city. Pontferrada takes its name from the *puente de ferro*, the 'iron bridge' across the Rio Sil, erected to help Compostela pilgrims at the end of the eleventh century. The Templars built a huge castle here to guard the crossing and it still overlooks the river, while the 'Catholic Kings', Ferdinand and Isabella, built a hostel, the Hospital de la Reina, in 1948, to celebrate the end of the *Reconquista*.

Poke about in the narrow back streets of Pontferrada as the shadows lengthen and the medieval world comes alive, especially if a Compostela-bound confraternity passes by in the dusk, singing away behind their banner.

*   *   *

Next day began pleasantly. A cool morning and a wide pilgrim-dotted road leading west into the wine country of the Bierzo. Here, closer to the wet Atlantic winds, the land is greener, and those flat, scorching grainlands of the Castilian *meseta* seemed a million miles away as I wound my way west, past Cacabelos where St Roch had a hermitage, and down to the town of Villafranca de Bierzo, an attractive town and a wine centre.

As the name indicates, Villafranca, the 'French town' was created by the pilgrim trade. Even the guide describes Villafranca as the *'hija* [daughter] *de la peregrinacion jacobea'*. It was founded in the eleventh century by the monks of Cluny, who built the first church here, Neustra Senora de Cluniaco, to mark the end of the tenth stage on the Road to Compostela. The main sights today are the castle of the Marquis del Bierzo, which dates from about 1490, and among many others, the eleventh-century church of Santiago, where by tradition any true pilgrim who had come this far and was physically unable to tackle the mountains of Galicia, could touch the *puerta del perdon*, the door of pardon at the church, and receive all the indulgences due to a true Santiago pilgrim. To give up here, with only 170km to go, must have been penance enough.

The Road crosses two rivers at Villafranca, the Valcarcel and the Burbia, and begins a long up-and-down passage, climbing steadily to the pass at Pedrafita, where I arrived, quite worn out, at about seven in the evening. Great thunderclouds were rolling in from the west, lightning flickered about the hills, and it seemed a good place to stop, so I was just about to give up and enter an hotel when, as so often on this journey, the three Viallard *gosses* appeared, skidding their bikes down the steep road from the hostel at El Cebrero. Up above, they implied, I could get a meal and sleep in the barn and, most important, catch up with them and the lady from Lyon. They looked expectant, so I tore myself away from the comforts of the hotel by the col, and trudged up on the mountain, through the wind, the gusts of rain and the gathering dusk, to the border of Léon and Galicia, into the light and warmth of the Hostel de San Giraldo, where Eve and the Viallards were waiting with some wine beside the fire. Once again our little *confrèrie* had come together.

*   *   *

El Cebrero has always been a famous spot on the *Camino Frances* and is the one which modern pilgrims will find most evocative of the pilgrim past. The present hotel and the church nearby were erected about the year 1072 by monks from the Abbey of St Gerald at Aurillac in France. In the fifteenth century the church gained even more fame when the Miracle of the Holy Eucharist took place here, another famous event in the history of the Pilgrim Road.

The story goes that one dark and stormy day in 1300, a peasant from a village nearby was the only one who came to hear Mass, served by a priest with very little faith in his mission. At the moment of consecration he had the unworthy thought, 'only a stupid peasant would come out on a day like this for some bread and a little wine'. Then, looking down, he discovered that the wine had indeed become blood, and the

Church at El Cebrero

bread flesh. The story of this miracle was spread far and wide by the pilgrims, and even brought Ferdinand and Isabella here on pilgrimage in 1486. The Chalice of the Miracle is still kept in the church at El Cebrero, and the services are always attended by the passing pilgrims.

Miracles apart, a hostel at El Cebrero would have been necessary anyway, for it is a bleak spot. On this particular night, in high summer, rain and sleet were dashed against the windows, and when the twins took me down to see the other pilgrims sleeping in the barn, we had to support each other against the violence of the wind. These barns are squat, thatched, stone structures called *pallozas*, and peculiar to Cebrero. During the height of the annual pilgrimage, they are crammed with travellers, and since the hostel was also full, I decided to erect my tent, which I managed with much assistance, in the lee of the churchyard wall. Dinner was a simple soup and stew, but the company was good. We were joined by a French priest, Father Denis from St Maur, a very cheery cleric, leading a group from his church on a foot pilgrimage to Compostela. I can never understand why many people are wary, even a little afraid of priests and monks. I have stayed at many monasteries over the years and have always found the residents to be the most cheerful souls, and Father Denis was a riot. Signing the pilgrim book at El Cebrero, I discovered that another British pilgrim was among that night's guests, a Welshman walking from Barcelona, but in the best traditions of the British abroad, we ignored each other and conversed, if at all, in Spanish.

During the night the storm blew itself out, and dawn was glorious here, high on the mountain, the sun striking down on great banks of white cloud that filled the valley far below. Everywhere the pilgrims were stirring, packing their rucksacks, setting off down the road. Having decided that we should stay together from now on we loaded our panniers into Isabelle's car, mounted our bikes and set out to climb yet again to the pass at Puyo. Up there we met Father Denis and his flock gathered in a group around a donkey. Denis was attired for the

Eve and the twins at Puyo

150

Road in black cassock, a rucksack, big boots and a straw sombrero. 'How do I look?' he asked. 'Ridiculous,' I told him.

* * *

From Puyo the Road falls away, first to Samos, where our pilgrim passports were stamped by the abbot at the monastery. Just before Samos the Road passes through the village of Triacastela. Although only two castles ever seem to have been built there, it was an important stop, the eleventh, for pilgrims and there is still a pilgrim monument beside the Road. In medieval times pilgrims would carry a stone from Triacastela to Casteñada near Mellid, where they would be ground into cement for the cathedral at Santiago, so small stones duly went into our pockets before we passed on across this ever greener

151

Romanesque fortified church at Puertomarin

and attractive countryside, through Sarria for our night stop at Puertomarin.

Sarria is overlooked by a castle and has several churches and hospitals linked to the pilgrim traffic, although Picaud does not mention it in his guide; but the up-and-down road to the west, lined with eucalyptus trees, and running through a lush countryside, is now well supplied with signs to Compostela.

We climbed our last hill that day, came round a corner and swooped down to the bridge over the Mino and into Puertomarin, a delightful town. Puertomarin has moved in recent years. When the Mino was dammed and the river rose, much of the old town would have disappeared unless parts of it, notably the church of St Nicolas, had not been moved higher up the hill. The stones were carefully numbered before the church was dismantled and moved uphill to its present position in the town centre. This church is Romanesque and

Welcome to Compostela

fortified with battlements, for it belonged originally to the Knights of St John. There is a *parador* at Puertomarin, a modern one overlooking the river, but they have a statue of St James in the hall, and a host of pilgrims were there for dinner, so nothing broke the mood as we set out with a host of other cyclists on the last 80km to Santiago. I did not want this journey to end, but the others were indifferent, so we poured out, yelling to each other, on this long final stage.

This road was crowded on that Monday morning, not just with pilgrims but with the country people going about their business, or travelling to market in those amazing Galician buses which have seats for passengers in the front and space for cattle at the rear, and go roaring past with a blast of petrol and manure. The locals were delighted to see the pilgrims and little groups stood in every garden, waving us down to take a glass of wine.

At Lestedo, turning a little off the road, we came to the quiet little church of the Knights of Santiago at Villar de Donas, built in 1184. This charming church is full of the tombs and tombstones of those knights who kept open the Road to St James, a romantic, rather sad spot, basking in the morning sunshine.

Palas do Rei, Picaud's twelfth stop on the Road, is very

small and crammed with pilgrims; we dumped our stones at Casteñada; Mellid has the churches of San Pedro and Santa Maria; Arzua is the last town of any size before Compostela, but we were now in a hurry, pressing on to the finish, encouraged by the ever-growing groups of pilgrims, that sense of excitement and a small sense of sadness that the end was in sight. Jacques' small triangles of cheese, handed out as *'bon pour la force'*, also helped us on the way.

Quite suddenly the road flattened out. A big jet, bearing the insignia of British Airtours, roared overhead, wheels down, coming into land at Lavacolla, the airport of Santiago. In former times, the pilgrims would halt to wash off the dirt of the journey in the spring at Lavacolla, but this has disappeared under the concrete runway, so we settled for a look at the Rio Lavacolla which runs under the road, before moving on for one final pilgrim ritual of the Road on the hill of Monte del Gozo, which lies just behind the little village of San Marcos by the Road, and offers the first view of Compostela.

> Upon a hill it stands on hie,
> Wher Sent Jamez first shalt thou see
> A Montjoie, many stones here att
> And four piles of stone of grate state
> A hundred daiz of pardon
> There may thou have . . . .

A hundred days of indulgence added to that remission of half the time in Purgatory due to any Compostela pilgrim is a bonus worth having.

Pilgrims would race up here from the Road, vying with each other for that first glimpse of the spires of Compostela, the winner shouting *'Montjoie'* at the sight. Whoever won the race to the top was declared the 'king' of that confraternity and thereafter named Le Roy. It did not seem right to compete when we had come all this way together, so we walked up, cresting the little hill together, and there it was before us, after a thousand miles across France and Spain. The spires of the Cathedral Church of Santiago de Compostela rose gleaming in the afternoon sun, marking the end of our journey. *Montjoie!*

Chapter 10
The City of St James

'What city is like unto this great city?'

Revelation 18:18

So we came at last to 'Compostela, the most excellent city of the Apostle, which has all manner of delights, and holds in custody the precious mortal remains of St James, for which reason it is rightly considered the most fortunate and exalted of all cities of Spain'.

Picaud could hammer out the felicitious phrase when he put his mind to it. We rode in through the usual suburbs and light industry clutter which surrounds any town today, following the crowds into the centre of the city, through the Puenta del Camino, dismounting to walk down the old streets beside the Cathedral, a route lined with stalls and shops, past the Palace of Gelmirez and round to the entrance of the Cathedral, facing the vast Plaza de Obradoiro, one of the finest squares in Spain. Pilgrims were everywhere, chatting in groups, squatting on their rucksacks, queuing on the Cathedral steps to finish their journey in the traditional way. Our bikes were chained to the railings and we climbed the steps of the Baroque façade which now conceals the old Romanesque Cathedral, and through the narthex to the Portico de la Gloria, the 'Door of Glory'. The central column of this door is the Pilgrim Pillar, where we took our turn to place our hands upon it as Santiago pilgrims have done for centuries, until the very stone is grooved with the pressure of countless fingers. This done, our pilgrimage was complete — or almost.

In the last weeks, the rhythm of the Road had carried us forward at a fair pace, missing none of the main sights perhaps, but still finding it necessary to press on and chalk up the necessary daily mileage. Now the journey was over, and we had time to look around.

The Portico de la Gloria, the Cathedral of Santiago de Compostela

Compostela *is* a fine city, with a centre which reflects the great glories of medieval Spain. In any other country such squares as they have in Compostela would only be found in the capital. The city dates from around the year 850, and grew up around the original Chapel of St James. That story of the *Campo-Stella,* the Field of Stars, is held here to be a legend, for excavtion under the cathedral in 1946 revealed a Roman necropolis, and *compostela* is also the Latin word for cemetery. The second, larger church on this site was destroyed by Al-Manzur, though he spared the Shrine of St James. When Al-Manzur rode into the basilica on 10 August 997, everyone had fled except an old monk who was kneeling by the Saint's tomb. 'And what are you doing here?' asked Al-Manzur. 'Are you not afraid?' 'I am the familiar of St James, and I am at my prayers,' replied the monk. Al-Manzur spared the shrine, from which the relics had, in fact, been removed, but he razed the church and the city to the ground. The bells were carried

The Cathedral of Santiago de Compostela

all the way back to Cordoba on the shoulders of his Christian prisoners, where, inverted and filled with oil, they served as lamps in the great mosque until St Ferdinand captured Cordoba in 1236 and *his* Moorish prisoners then carried the bells back again to Compostela.

By and large though, and when not actually on campaign, the Moorish rulers were tolerant of the Christian religion, and allowed their Christian subjects a considerable degree of freedom, although they were not allowed to ride horses, had to pay a special tax, and were forbidden to ring their church bells within earshot of any mosque. The present cathedral was built in stages, as the pilgrim traffic grew, so that it contains elements from the eleventh, twelfth and thirteenth centuries. To accommodate even larger crowds than the building itself could contain, the cathedral is surrounded by squares, so that large as it is, it appears enormous, overtopping the town.

The Bishop of Compostela was much more than a cleric. He

ruled in hard times, was responsible for one of the great shrines, and exercised greater influence than Diego Gelmirez, *'Obispo de Santiage, con baculo y ballesta'*, Bishop of St James 'with crozier and crossbow'.

Gelmirez came to Compostela in 1095 as assistant to the Cluniac bishop, Dalmatius, and became a bishop of the diocese in 1100. Gelmirez was a businessman, and a warlike cleric. He got a firm grip on the lax brotherhood of monks, forcing them to shave, forbidding them to come to the church booted and spurred — one cannot but wonder what monastic life was like here in the years before 1100. It is said that the monks 'hated him quite wonderfully'. Gelmirez began a programme of building and rebuilding, opened hostels for the pilgrim trade, and did all he could to spread the word about the shrine and encourage the pilgrimage.

In 1104, Bishop Gelmirez set out for Rome, pausing on the way at Cluny to see the abbot St Hugh and enlist his support in raising Compostela to an archbishopric, and returned from the Papal see with the pallium. Much of what we know of Compostela we owe to Gelmirez. He made the shrine famous, encouraged Picaud in the writing of his Guide, and raised money for Santiago from every noble house in Europe. He died in 1139, and is buried in the cathedral cloisters.

*   *   *

Having arrived in Compostela, the true pilgrim still has much to do. Our journey completed, the Pilgrim Pillar touched, and our respects to St James having been paid, we now had to obtain our *compostelles*. These we obtained from a priest in the Cathedral secretariat, a jolly fellow in a black cassock bearing the red cross of Santiago, who inspected our pilgrim passports, and filled in our *compostelles*, tapping out the details on an old typewriter. These declared that we had completed the 'true pilrimage of St James' and were therefore entitled to all the privileges of a true pilgrim.

'But how,' I asked him, 'can you tell a "true pilgrim" from a mere tourist or coach traveller? Not all get their passports from

French pilgrims arrive in Santiago de Compostela

Madame Debril, not all come by St Jean?'

'We can always tell a "true pilgrim",' he said. 'They have a look about them.' I took a glance at the others as we walked back across the cloister and indeed, they had a look about them. A little weary and worn from the Road perhaps, but healthy, sunburnt, happy, even a touch exalted. I wondered if I, too, had 'the look' about me.

These *compostelles* were useful documents, much more than souvenirs. On the way home they would give the pilgrim freedom from tolls, and admit him to pilgrim hostels. They also proved that he or she had actually completed the journey, which was particularly useful to those who undertook the journey as an act of judicial punishment. A pilgrimage was often used as a banishment, a kind of probation, and this custom, too, has not entirely died out. Only the day before, two Belgian delinquents had arrived, after walking all the way from Liege, accompanied by a policeman. A magistrate had offered them the choice of a year in prison or the pilgrimage to Compostela for setting fire to cars but when they brought him their *compostelles*, their slate was clean.

One of the other privileges of the true pilgrim is the right to

Hostel de los Reyes Catolicos, from the Cathedral

The façade of Hostal de los Reyes Catolicos

free meals for three days at the Hostel de los Reyes Catolicos, now a luxury hotel which lies just acros the square from the Cathedral. Present your *compostelle* here and they must feed you, but since they keep the *compostelle*, which true pilgrims treasure, wise ones present a photocopy. Emerging from the Puerta Santa, the Holy Door, which is only open during Holy Years, we made our way across the Plaza de la Quintana to the Plaza de las Platerias, the Square of the Silversmiths, a place lined with jewellery shops, and into the Rua del Villar, where a photography shop duly copied our *compostelles*.

'Now I need a drink,' declared Jacques. He had been saying that at regular intervals for nearly a month, and as Jacques and Isabelle were old Compostela hands, he led us directly to Suso's. Señor Suso, and his bar, are famous among the true pilgrims. His little hotel and restaurant are tucked away under the arches down the Rua del Villar, and he keeps open house for the true pilgrims, with good food, comfortable beds, moderate prices and the theory that there is always room for one more. He greeted the Viallards like long-lost relatives, shook hands with all around, and showed us his vast collection of postcards, which pour in from all over the world — his own confraternity, '*Los Amigos de Suso*'.

Just across the Rua, in the Oficina de Turismo, works another good friend, Señor Ballesteros, the manager of the office, and since the Viallards were already booked in at Suso's, and the city was full of pilgrims in this Holy Year, Eve and I went across to beg his assistance. Within an hour we had found somewhere to stay, dumped the bikes, taken off our dusty, sweaty cycling clothes and were ready to explore the city as it worked itself into a climax for the feast day of St James.

* * *

The Plaza de Obradoiro, where much of the festivities take place, must be one of the most beautiful squares in the world, surrounded by fine buildings, the great Cathedral, the long elegant façade of the Hostel de los Reyes Catolicas, the Palacio del Rajoy, which serves as the Town Hall and has elegant

Puerta Santa, the Holy Door opened only during Holy Years

public rooms, and the Colegio de San Jeronimo. Standing in the middle of the square, everything falls into proportion and the sense of space is marvellous.

Pilgrims would enter the city, as we had done, through what was the Porta Françigena, the French Gate, now the Puerta del Camino, and make their way on foot to the cathedral. Now that we had completed the pilgrimage we took a little more time to study the building before joining the congregation for one of the pilgrim services which are held throughout the week, and the flight of the *botafumeiro*.

The rain that sweeps across Galicia, that rain we were currently spared, has done wonders to the Cathedral façade. This ornate baroque facing, full of carving and statues, encrusted with ironwork, has become a garden in the rain, with grass, flowers, and even small shrubs sprouting from every crevice. On this evening much of the façade was hidden behind scaffolding, ready for the great firework display that

Plaza de Obradoira, Santiago de Compostela

concludes the festivities.

We went inside for another look at the Portico de la Gloria, that great carved doorway, the work of Maestro Mateo. It is a masterpiece, endlessly intricate, a Tree of Jesse in which Santiago replaces the more usual statue of the Virgin or Christ. Mateo was a Frenchman, one of those wandering freemasons, and he worked in the cathedral for at least fifty years, from 1168 until 1217. His own humble little statue behind the pillar, now well worn by time, is the one which receives the head-tappings from the pilgrims, and is known therefore as the *Santo dos Croques*, the Saint of the Skull-taps.

Marin appeared while we were inspecting all this and led us back outside. 'The French are coming,' he said, pointing across the square. 'We have met an English girl who has walked here all the way from your Canterbury. Her French is much better than yours,' he added, pointedly.

The large French group now coming towards the Cathedral behind the banners of their confraternity, and the *fleurs-de-lys semelée* banner of the French cavalry, were from Les Amis de St Jacques in Paris, led on this occasion by the president, the Marquis de la Coste-Messelière, their secretary Mademoiselle Warcollier, and this English girl, Jocelyn Rix, last heard of from Madame Debril at St Jean. Like myself, she had clearly

Jocelyn Rix at Compostela, after walking from Canterbury

become an honorary *Française*, for she was carrying their banner. Their little service in one of the side chapels preceded the much longer one in the main body of the Cathedral, which included a fine welcoming sermon from the archbishop and concluded with that popular compostela attraction, the *botafumeiro*.

The *botafumeiro*, the 'Great Censer of St James', is only deployed on special occasions. It is the largest censer in the world, standing some six feet in height and when in use hangs on a rope which descends from a pulley set over a hundred feet high in the transept of the church. Six men carry it in, smoking lightly, hook it to the rope and haul it up. Then they start it swinging, to and fro, higher and higher, smoke and sparks flying, a low rising moan from the wind venting through the holes as this great glittering object sweeps in a huge arc across the cathedral, only inches over the heads of the marvelling congregation; God's Exocet! When it finally stopped, after the air inside had been filled with blue clouds of incense, I rather expected applause. I managed to see three flights of the

botafumeiro during my stay in Compostela, and each one was a show-stopper.

As to the sermon, I have no notes, but it was all that such a sermon should have been, said before that vast, sunburnt and travel-stained congregation, a speech of welcome and encouragement. Had we not found that there was still virtue in the pilgrimage, still friendship on the Road? Had we not discovered that 'the Way of St James is fine but narrow, as narrow as the path to Salvation?' The archbishop concluded by inviting us to shake hands all round, after which the crowd surged cheerfully out into the Plaza de Obradoiro, many heading determinedly for Suso's, while Eve and I went off for a look at the Hostel de los Reyes Catolicos.

This splendid hotel began life six centuries ago as yet another pilgrim hostel built by the Knights of Santiago, and one almost as splendid as the San Marcos. It passed into the hands of Ferdinand and Isabella when they extinguished the Order in 1498 but it remained a pilgrim hostel, and maintained the knightly rule of offering hospitality to anyone bearing a *compostelle*, an obligation which the present management took over when the hostel was converted into a luxury hotel in the 1950s. They have since narrowed their commitment down to one meal per person, and a maximum of ten pilgrims per meal, and serve it in a small room just off the kitchens, but I hope the custom continues. I enjoyed watching the more elegant guests stepping delicately aside to let· the 'true pilgrims' pile up their rucksacks in the foyer, and be led upstairs to dine.

* * *

Arriving early at Compostela left us with a few days to spare before the Feast of St James, so we rode out on the following day to the final place of obligation at the little port of Padron, the former *Iria Flavia*, where the body of St James floated ashore all those centuries ago. Padron lies in one of the Galician *rias* or estuaries, 20km south of Compostela. These

Statue of St James in the Portico de la Gloria

rias indent the coast deeply, and are quite beautiful, at least when the tide is in and covering a vast amount of refuse.

Padron is just a little place, at the head of the Ria de Arosa. Like Oviedo, all Compostela pilgrims should go there for:

Quien voy a Santiago e non va al Padron
O faz Romeria, o non

— which I think explains itself. A large flat stone on the beach is said to be all that remains of the saint's boat, and there is a little chapel to the saint, but it is not really a place at which to linger. We went on, south along the *rias*, to the *parador* at Cambados, before riding back to Compostela, and the great Feast Day of St James.

*   *   *

The Day of St James began with pipes and drum. I leaned out of the bedroom window and watched the folklore groups of Galicia flooding down the Rua del Villar by the score, each led by Galician bagpipes and drums, most of the players in national costume, all heading for the Plaza de Obradoiro, or the folklorique competitions which went on all day for the next twenty-four hours, and the sound dins in my ears still.

Since it was his *Santo* as well, we hurried out to find Jacques, and rounded up the Viallards for a celebration lunch of *coquille St Jacques*, or *vieras* as they call them locally. Armand, inevitably, had a large tortilla, while Eve's speciality was *freisas con nata*, or strawberries in whipped cream. We all had rather too much Rioja. The afternoon was spent watching the dancing in the plaza and the periodic passing of Juan Carlos, the King of Spain, heading for the cathedral or various foundations round the town. The day concluded with that spectacular, long-promised firework display, when the fireworks set all over the cathedral façade, blazed into a brief life, a marvellous sight to see, even when crushed among the crowd of thousands in the square below; we eased our way free and went to join the pilgrims in Suso's.

All the fellowship of the Road was in Suso's that night;

Father Denis, the Viallards, Jocelyn Rix the girl from Wolverhampton, her brother Paddy who had walked with her from Pontferrada, Miguel and Santi, grinning from ear to ear — all the pilgrims we had met along the Road.

'Those girls over there seem to know you from somewhere,' said Eve, pointing out three pretty girls, waving from the corner. 'I don't know them, but I recognise their dog,' I replied, waving back a welcome to the students last seen at San Isidro. The noise was tremendous and Senor Suso was in his element, stacking up bottles on the bar, adding more people to the membership of *Los Amigos de Suso*.

Sometime after midnight we went back to the Plaza de Obradoiro, along streets suddenly quiet and empty after the crowds and bustle of the day. The square was deserted except for the occasional hurrying figure and quiet except for the distant sound of pipe and drum; the damp air smelled faintly of fireworks. Eve and I sat on the steps of the Cathedral and relaxed.

'Were I the romantic type,' I said at last, 'I could say that I imagine this place full of ghosts, the ghosts of all those millions of pilgrims who have followed the Way of St James. The lucky ones might even play their cards right and beg time out of Heaven to be here tonight. It would be a pity to miss such a party.'

'Is that how you feel?' she asked. 'Cynical about it all.?'

'No, I don't,' I said. 'I'm not at all cynical. I feel sorry that the journey is over, but glad that I came. I got something out of the pilgrimage; just what, I haven't yet decided, but I feel good about it.

'How can there be ghosts?' said the ever-practical Eve. 'To be a ghost you must be dead, and the pilgrimage is not dead, you know that. I'm sorry this journey is over, but there are many roads to St James. After all, we can always come again. Why not next year...?'

So we went back across the Plaza, past the great church where the Apostle still sleeps, rejoin that cheerful group of friends who had come with us all the way down that hard, hot and glorious Road that comes out of the past, and leads to Compostela.

Bibliography

Iberia, James Michener (Fawcett Crest, New York)
Priez pour nous a Compostelle, * Barret et Gurgand (Hachette & Livre de Poche, 1977)
The Song of Roland, edited by E.V. Rieu (Penguin)
El Camino de Santiago, * E.G. Arronto (Editorial Everest, Madrid)
Vers Compostelle, Janine Ducrot (Editions NEL, France)
The Way of St James, T.A. Layton (George Allan & Unwin, 1976)
The Age of Chivalry, Arthur Bryant (Collins, 1963)
Le Guide du Pelerin de St Jacques de Compostelle, * (Liber Santi Jacobi of Ameri Picaud) translated by Jeanne Valliard (Imprimer Protat Freres, Maçon)
Corunna, Christopher Hibbert (Batsford, 1961)
Confession of St Augustine, edited by E.V. Rieu (Penguin Classics)
St Jacques et les Chemins de Compostelle, * Jean Secret (Editions Fernand Lanore, Paris)
Pelerins du Moyen Age, Raymond Oussel (Editions Fayard, Paris)
En Vacances sur le Chemin de Compostelle, Rene Brynoert (Editions Duculot)
The Canterbury Tales, Geoffrey Chaucer (Penguin Classics)
Guia del Peregrino et Camino de Santiago, * (published by Ministerio de Transportes, Turismo y Communicaciones, Madrid)
The Reconquest of Spain, D.W. Lomox (Longman, 1978)
Pilgrimage: An Image of Medieval Religion, * Johnathan Sumption (Faber, 1975)
English Heraldry, Boutell (Frederick Warne, 1984)
The Way of St James (3 volumes), Professor Georgina King (New York)
The Pilgrimage to Santiago, * Edwin Mullins (Secker & Warburg, 1974)
Spain in the Middle Ages, Angus Mackay (Macmillan, 1977)
In Search of the Cid, * Stephen Clissold (Hodder & Stoughton, 1965)
Spain, Michelin Green Guide (in English) (1974)
The Cult of Santiago, J.S. Stone (Longman, 1927)
The Way to Santiago (pamphlet published by The Spanish National Tourist Office)
The Road to Santiago, * Walter Starkie (John Murray, 1957)
Spain, Jan Morris (Penguin)
The Waning of the Middle Ages, * J. Huizinga (Penguin)

— and for *true pilgrims*:

Cycletouring in France, Rob Hunter (Muller, 1984)
Richard's Bicycle Book, Richard Benjamin (Pan)

* denotes those titles which are particularly useful

Appendix I

SOURCES OF INFORMATION

Those planning to follow one of the four Roads to Compostela from Le Puy, Arles, Paris or Vézelay, will find much useful information by contacting the following sources:

The French Government Tourist Office,
178 Piccadilly,
London W1V 0AL
Tel: 01 493 6911

The Spanish National Tourist Office,
57 St James Street,
London SW1
Tel: 01 499 0901

The Confraternity of St James in England,
57 Leopold Road,
London N2
Tel: 01 883 4893

Les Amis de St Jacques,
(Secretary: Mlle J. Warcollier),
4 Square du Pont de Sevres,
92100 Boulogne sur Seine,
(Nr Paris)
Tel: (010) 33 605 80 50

Appendix II

EQUIPMENT FOR THE CYCLE-TOURIST

The cycle-tourist planning to follow the Road to Compostela needs a good 10- or 15-speed touring cycle. I recommend either the Raleigh 15 'Classic', or one of the excellent touring machines built by F.W. Evans of The Cut, London SE1.

KIT: The rule is simple — the less the better. Take clothing on the one-on, one-off, one-for-the-wash principle. Each day's clothing can be washed in the evening. Shampoo can be used for washing clothes as well as the hair. My kit list for the trip was as follows:

To Wear:
- 1   tee-shirt
- 1   neckerchief
- 1   pair Rohan shorts
- 1   pair underpants
- 1   pair socks
- 1   pair trainers
- 1   handkerchief
- 1   pair gloves
- 1   pair sunglasses

Clothing carried:
- 1   Rohan Pampas jacket
- 2   tee-shirts
- 2   pairs underpants
- 2   pairs socks
- 1   pair shorts
- 1   pair cotton trousers
- 1   pair Rohan trousers
- 2   handkerchiefs
- 1   wind- and waterproof jacket
- 1   sun hat

Toilet and medical:
Lip salve
Sun cream
Washing and shaving gear
First-aid kit (aspirin, plasters, etc)
Bottle shampoo
Towel

Camping equipment:
- 1   Robert Saunders Jet Packer tent
- 1   Black's Icelandic sleeping bag
- 1   Thermarest self-inflating mattress
- 1   Trangia kettle and cook-pot
- 1   Camping Gaz Globe Trotter stove
- 2   spare cartridges
Knife, fork, spoon
Bottle opener

Trip equipment:
Passport
Tickets
Money
UK chequebook
Pens
- 1   Nikon FM2 SLR camera with 1 x 43-85mm zoom lens
- 1   Olympus 35mm RC camera
- 4   rolls (36) Kodak 64 film

4   rolls (36) Ilford 125 film

Cycle tools and spares:
2   spare inners
1   spare cover
6   spare spokes
1   rear brake cable
1   rear gear cable

Puncture repair outfit,
   spoke key
Pliers, screwdriver,
   multi-spanner
Allum keys, security chain with
   combination lock,
2 shock-cords

All this went very easily into two Karrimor 'Iberian' panniers and a handlebar bag.

Appendix III

ACCOMMODATION

There is no shortage of accommodation on the Roads to Compostela, but some hotels or *hostals* are particularly popular with 'true pilgrims'. The following lie along the Road from Le Puy.

FRANCE

Hotel du Grand Cerf
Le Puy

Hotel la Vieille Auberge
St Privat d'Allier

Hotel Sarda
Monistral d'Allier

Hotel de la Terrasse
Saugues

Hotel du Centre
St Alban sur Limagole

Grand Hotel de la Gare
Aumont-Aubrac

Hotel de la Route d'Argent
Nasbinals

Hotel du Centre
Aubrac

Hotel Vayrou
St Chely d'Aubrac

Hotel des Voyageurs
St-Côme-sur-Olt

Aux Armes d'Estaing
Estaing
or
Hotel Renaldy
Estaing

Hotel Ste Foy
Conques (expensive)
or
Hotel le Castellou
Conques

Hotel Terminus St Jacques
Figeac

Hotel Melchoir
Cahors

Hotel Chapon Fin
Moissac

Hotel Marechal-Foch
Condom

Hotel Henri IV
Eauze

Hotel Maugouler
Maslacq, near Orthez

Hotel Trinquet
St Palais

Hotel des Pyrenees
St-Jean-Pied-de-Port

SPAIN

Casa Sabina
Roncesvalles

Hostal Burguete
Burguete

Beti-Fai
Aoiz

Hostal Ibarra
Pamplona

Hostal Peregrino
Puente la Reina

Hotel Monaco
Los Arcos

Parador
Santo Domingo de la Calzada
(expensive)

Hostal Santa Teresita
Santo Domingo

Hotel Cordon
Burgos

Restaurant Anton
Castelgeriz

Hostal San Martin
Fromista

Meson Pisarrosas
Carrion de los Condes

Residencia Estrella
Masilla de los Mulas

Hotel San Marcos
Leon
(expensive)
or
Hostal Lambas
Leon

Hostal Gallego
Astorga

Hostal San Jorge
Ponferrada

Parador
Villafranca del Bierzo

El Cebrero
Hostal St Gerand al Aurrillac

Parador
Puerto Marin
or
Fonda del Camino
Puerto Marin

Hotel Suso
rua del Villar
Santiago de Compostela

Index